Such a Time

Alma,
May you learn to
be His Girl and live
with passion, vision, and
purpose.

Samantha

SAMANTHA ROOSE

SUCH A TIME

ISBN-13: 978-1522957669

ISBN-10: 1522957669

To my *Mom*, who has been committed to me living my "such a time" even when I lost the passion, vision, and purpose.

To *Emily Croft* who inspired me to make my journey more than a personal journey, but a journey other girls can learn from as well.

To *Jesus Christ*, without whom "such a time" would never exist.

CONTENTS

INTRO

Do you feel like your life is a five thousand-piece puzzle that came without a picture on the box?

Are you overwhelmed by having to fit together all of life's big decisions?

Have you been waiting for just the right moment for life to burst into color and perfection?

If so, then believe me — you're not alone!

When I graduated high school, I didn't know what to do or where to start. I felt like I should have at least known what my puzzle looked like before I could understand how to put it together. Instead, I felt like I was staring at a black-and-white, five thousand-piece puzzle without the box to guide me. So, not only was I trying to put together this masterpiece puzzle, but I didn't even know what it was supposed to look like, where to start, or how to put it together.

SUCH A TIME

So, like Rapunzel in her tower, I stared at it. Hour after hour. Tear after tear. I stared, intimidated by the senseless pieces, waiting for *someday when* they would all make sense. Then, one day, while those puzzling pieces were staring me down, I realized that the problem wasn't a black-and-white puzzle with no picture that was leaving me directionless.

The problem was my **staring** instead of **starting**.

The problem was that *someday when* would never come. While it kept my hopes up, *someday when* was just a fairytale. The answer was *today*. Real life was *this moment*. My *such a time* was here!

So, I did it. Tentatively, I extended my arm and picked up the first pieces.

I wish I could say that when I picked up the first pieces they fit together perfectly — they didn't. So I picked up another. After examining this one from all angles, I replaced it and chose another. Some pieces fit, others didn't. Piece after piece. Day after day. I try my best to make sense of the squiggly, scattered pieces.

Weeks come and go. Finally, months become years. There have been seasons of frustration and seasons of exhilaration, seasons of waiting and seasons of sprinting. But, like a tree over the course of a year, each season brings a beauty all its own. And each season teaches me more of what it means to be truly satisfied and successful as "His Girl."

I have often felt that I am blindly completing a connect-the-dot picture. All the pieces don't fit exactly the way I want, and the dots seem to create lopsided creations. Along the way, I have had to stop working on some sections to focus on others.

But today I've taken a step back, and do you know what I see? I see the first glimmer of a masterpiece. I see little black specks in a sea of white connecting to create an impressive tree that is confident of its identity and existence. I see a forest of dreams-turned-reality and stepping stones leading off the unfinished part of the puzzle. I can only imagine what magnificent view will emerge as I continue.

That's what this book is about—taking the scattered pieces of your life and fitting them together to make a masterpiece that glorifies God.

Throughout these pages, I'll teach you the significance of living for *such a time* and the dangers of waiting for *someday when.* I'll show you how to look at each piece from a different angle and fit it together with the next. Like a big sister, I'll help you identify the dots in your life and choose which ones to connect next. But, best of all, I'll give you an outline to the puzzle of your life so that you are not staring at five thousand little pieces with no direction.

I promise that all those squiggly, scattered, senseless pieces make sense — when you **stop staring** and **start creating**.

So don't stop here with epic words and inspirational phrases floating through your brain, waiting for *someday when* the time is right. I challenge you to seize your *such time,* pick up the first piece of your five thousand-piece puzzle, and make your life a masterpiece — by reading this book.

Actually, I dare you to finish the book! That's right, the book was written to come as a complete package — it's not a doughnut with a hole in the middle — so read all the way to the end!

And, when you get to the end, send me a an email telling me how this book changed your life, and I'll email you back!

SOMEDAY WHEN

Now is the time of God's favor, now is the day of salvation.
~2 Corinthians 6:2~

I love seasons. Living in Virginia is my favorite because I get all four seasons in unavoidable intensity. But fall has always been my favorite — fall fashion, especially, and the trees. Driving to Lynchburg this weekend, I couldn't help but notice the highways edged with leafy flames.

I realized that if it were always autumn, I would not love this season the way I do. And that's when I knew that not having autumn all year long was what made autumn so special. When summer shines bright, I wear my white capris whenever I'm not wearing workout clothes and make a strawberry smoothie every other night. But when fall burns on every tree, I am the first to zip up my boots, wrap my hands around a steaming cup of coffee, and curl up with a book.

Staring out the window at our backyard full of leaves and empty trees with a cup of coffee in my hands, I realized that life isn't all that much unlike the seasons of nature.

Have you ever wondered what makes today so special? Why is singleness special? Why is marriage special? What makes coming home from vacation almost as exciting as vacation itself? Why is going to college or staying at home special? What makes sibling relationships or selling things on Etsy special?

Before reading my friend's article, three years ago, these thoughts had never crossed my mind. I continually lived in a when-I-get married-life-will-be-special mindset. You could call it the "Olaf Complex" — *When I finally do what married girls do in marriage!* That's not to say that I thought all my problems would suddenly evaporate. I'm well aware of the difficulties accompanied with loving a man, running a household, and raising children. But, it was as though being married would finally make me feel like I had arrived! In short, I was always living for fall and never wearing my white capris and enjoying the strawberry smoothie.

When I finished reading the following article, I could see light at the end of the tunnel — a tunnel I had never realized I was in. Those faint glimmers drew me on a journey, a journey that changed the trajectory of my life and inspired me to host a conference, which led to my writing this book.

SUCH A TIME

So, without further ado . . .

Sometimes it seems like just a few weeks ago that I donned a beautiful, white dress and pledged my life to the man of my dreams. Then again, sometimes it seems like we have been married forever, and it is hard to imagine life before Nathan Britton became such an important part of my world.

In reality, it has now been four months since we promised to love and cherish one another until death do us part. Four months of wonder and bliss, as well as the challenges of learning and adjustment that come when two lives become one. Oh yes, and four months of change — lots of change. In the short time we have been married, I have become pregnant with our first child and we have moved to a new state where Nathan has taken on a new job as the senior pastor of a small church. Life is certainly never dull! Though change and transition are not always easy, I can honestly say that we are loving every minute of the continuous adventures we are experiencing!

Now that our house is almost finished being painted and most of our boxes are unpacked, I have finally had the chance to slow down and reflect a little on all that has happened in my life of late. I am realizing that the changes that have been taking place are not only external, circumstantial changes, but also those of priority, perspective, and responsibility.

For many years, 1 Corinthians 7:34 has been like a compass for me, pointing me in the right direction and giving me purpose and focus, first as a single girl, and now as a married woman. It says this:

SUCH A TIME

> There is a difference also between a wife and a virgin. The unmarried woman cares for the things of the Lord, that she may be holy both in body and in spirit; but she that is married cares for the things of the world, how she may please her husband.

During my teen years and early twenties, it was my goal to be that unmarried woman who cared for the things of the Lord.

A girl's single years afford her, like no other time, the opportunity to really cultivate a close, intimate walk with the Savior. Unattached from the full responsibilities of a home and husband and children, she has the time to dig into deep Bible study, to journal things God is teaching her if she is so inclined, to spend much time in prayer, and to pour out her life in ministry as God opens doors. While marriage is a good thing to desire and prepare for, the unmarried woman shouldn't waste her life pining for her prince and dawdling the days away wondering when he will come, but instead, to focus her energies on loving Jesus and serving others in a way that will honor Him.

The second part of a single girl's focus, being holy both in body and in spirit, simply means living a set-apart life in accordance with the holiness and righteousness Christ has given her; choosing a lifestyle that reflects His character instead of the corruption and vain pursuits of the world.

I am so grateful that God gave me this verse as a lifeline to cling to during my single years because it helped me to live those years to the fullest. When the time for marriage did come, I was able to look back with no regrets on the season of singleness God had given me.

Now that I am married, the truths of the second half of 1 Corinthians 7:34 have become very real to me. I have a new focus and purpose: to care for the practical "things of the world" — laundry, dishes, meals, grocery shopping, the responsibilities of a house, etc. — and to seek to please my husband. This is not to say that with a shift in focus I have suddenly stopped "caring for the things of the Lord," but simply that the way I care for the things that please Him is different than it was when I was single (i.e., by honoring my husband, I honor Him). The way my time is spent is also different. I don't have the time like I used to for long periods of daily Bible study, or skill building, or devoting months on end in a foreign country to care for orphans.

Now, my days are consumed with tending to my husband and home and being available for the things he wants me to do as his helpmeet in life. Sometimes this means staying up late at night to read together, or going on an appointment with him, or watching a football game (not my favorite activity in the world, I assure you, but much more enjoyable when at his side!). It means planning meals according to his tastes, being ready to extend hospitality at the drop of a hat, serving alongside him in church ministry, and striving to be cheerful when I would just rather be grumpy. (Because after all, who wants to be married to a grump?) Pleasing my husband has become my new focus, and it's wonderful and challenging in its own way, just like being unmarried was wonderful and challenging in a different kind of way!

So why do I write all this for you to read today? What's the point?

Well, I am guessing based on the readership of this magazine (Inside Out), that many (if not most) of you find yourselves yet in the season of singleness, and I want to be of encouragement especially to you. Perhaps (and hopefully), one day you will experience the joys of being married to a man of God and serving alongside him in this life. But until that day comes, please realize what a gift you have been given in this season that you have to "care for the things of the Lord" as an unmarried woman. It is not a time to mope or sit around idly waiting for a husband to show up. You have time and availability now that you may not ever have in the same way again! Live these years to the absolute fullest! Cultivate a love relationship with Christ, choose a lifestyle that reflects His holiness, diligently attend to your studies, serve your family with gladness, build important skills that will come in handy in life, and actively engage in ministry opportunities that will open doors to share the Gospel.

If you do, God will be honored, for you will be walking according to His Word, and you will be able to look back on your single years with deep satisfaction and no regrets! (Katrina Britton, "Reflections from a Newly Wed," InsideOut, September 12, 2012)

Singleness—an *opportunity* . . . seriously? Look back on my single years with *satisfaction*? Suddenly, my world was rocked, and, for the first time, I noticed the streams of light in that tunnel I didn't even know that I was in. Questions overwhelmed me as I began walking toward those flickers of light. Was I always going to live for *someday when* . . .?

Someday when I graduate . . .

SUCH A TIME

Someday when I get married . . .
Someday when I have my dream job . . .
Someday when I have kids . . .
Someday when . . .

When I finally stepped out from the damp, depressing darkness into the brilliant, promising light, I felt free, excited about life, and filled with purpose. My soul was standing at the mouth of the tunnel with my arms outstretched, breathing in deeply the freshness of hope.

Taking in the view of lush hills and clear blue skies, I couldn't imagine why I would want to wait for another *someday*. Instead, I wanted to run fiercely into that gorgeous open space and savor it. I didn't want to miss my opportunity and regret not taking advantage of the abundant place God had brought me to.

Enough waiting in the hopelessly endless tunnel for *someday when* . . . Walking into the light, I realized that *someday when* doesn't exist. It's a figment of our imaginations—a distant date that never sends you off into the sunset with Prince Charming.

Instead, I found *such a time*. And, *such a time* does exist. It's today, right now, this very moment.

Such a time is a dare, an opportunity, and a responsibility: a dare to live a life of memories instead of regrets, an opportunity to invest in others, and a responsibility to glorify God. That's what Paul was saying:

> An unmarried woman or virgin is concerned about the Lord's affairs: Her aim is to be devoted to the Lord in both body and spirit. But a married woman is concerned about the affairs of this world — how she can please her husband. I am saying this for your own good, not to restrict you, but that you may live in a right way in undivided devotion to the Lord.
>
> (1 Corinthians 7:34–35)

There is beauty today, in the here and now, whether married or single, but each season's beauty is different. In singleness, the beauty today is my freedom to go where and when I want, and serve with all that I am without worrying about preparing dinner for my husband or tucking my children into bed. In marriage, the beauty today is serving everyday, rain or shine, loving my husband and nurturing my children.

I think that's what Paul is trying to say, "I am saying this for your own good, not to restrict you, but that you may live in a right way in undivided devotion to the Lord."

Just as each season of nature has beauty all its own, so do the seasons in my life. If in the winter I stay inside the whole time, waiting for new green buds to sprout, I will miss the glistening branches. If I complain every moment I'm at the beach, telling everyone how invigorating autumn is with its brilliant colors and crisp air, I miss the opportunity to feel the sun on my skin and sand in between my toes as I chase my siblings in the salty waves.

It's the same with seasons in life. If I'm single and always dreaming about getting married, filling up my "going to the chapel" Pinterest board, and making a mental list of my children-to-be names, I miss the opportunity to build relationships with my siblings and influence my community. If, when I'm married, all I can think about is all the things I will do when my children graduate or I long for my single days once again, I'm missing the moments I get to slather sunscreen on my children at the beach (the days I so recently dreamed of, remember?). When I'm always living for autumn to set the trees aflame or *someday when* to arrive, I miss living today in the "right way" because I'm focused on tomorrow's season.

I don't know about you, but I want to "live in a right way." And I think that begins with realizing that *such a time* is today. It's not tomorrow or when I get a real job. *Such a time* does not begin when I get married or finally have toddlers who can say "Mommy." My *such a time* is now. Today. This very moment. After all, if God created today, something tells me He's not waiting to be glorified *someday when* . . .

Invest Today

In the end we are more restricted when we live for *someday when* because *someday when* never comes. Instead of walking straight through to the light at the end of the tunnel and living purposefully, we walk in circles while we wait for our purpose to arrive. We are acting like the man who was given one talent:

> [14] Again, it will be like a man going on a journey, who called his servants and entrusted his wealth to them. [15] To one he gave five bags of gold, to another two bags, and to another one bag, each according to his ability. Then he went on his journey. [16] The man who had received five bags of gold went at once and put his money to work and gained five bags more. [17] So also, the one with two bags of gold gained two more. [18] But the man who had received one bag went off, dug a hole in the ground and hid his master's money.
>
> [19] After a long time the master of those servants returned and settled accounts with them. [20] The man who had received five bags of gold brought the other five. "Master," he said, "you entrusted me with five bags of gold. See, I have gained five more."
>
> [21] His master replied, "Well done, good and faithful servant! You have been faithful with a few things; I will put you in charge of many things. Come and share your master's happiness!"

²² The man with two bags of gold also came. "Master," he said, "you entrusted me with two bags of gold; see, I have gained two more."

²³ His master replied, "Well done, good and faithful servant! You have been faithful with a few things; I will put you in charge of many things. Come and share your master's happiness!"

²⁴ Then the man who had received one bag of gold came. "Master," he said, "I knew that you are a hard man, harvesting where you have not sown and gathering where you have not scattered seed. ²⁵ So I was afraid and went out and hid your gold in the ground. See, here is what belongs to you."

²⁶ His master replied, "You wicked, lazy servant! So you knew that I harvest where I have not sown and gather where I have not scattered seed? ²⁷ Well then, you should have put my money on deposit with the bankers, so that when I returned I would have received it back with interest.

²⁸ "So take the bag of gold from him and give it to the one who has ten bags. ²⁹ For whoever has will be given more, and they will have an abundance. Whoever does not have, even what they have will be taken from them. ³⁰ And throw that worthless servant outside, into the darkness, where there will be weeping and gnashing of teeth." (Matthew 25:14–30)

Instead of burying our talent in the ground or walking in circles in a hopelessly endless tunnel, God asks us to invest. The man who had been given one talent had his purpose staring him in face, but, like many of us, he decided to wait for *someday when*. And *someday when* — never came.

Finally, the master returned and asked what had been done with what he had trusted to his servants. The man with the single talent, which he had buried, was thrown out for not investing his master's money. While the other two men who had merely doubled the master's talents were rewarded and given more.

Neither the man with five talents nor the man with two talents went out to find more talents to invest. They simply invested what they had been given and were rewarded for it. So — stop wandering in circles looking for more talents to invest.

The purpose of living our *such a time* is to glorify God with what we have been given. We live with no regrets when we invest everything God has given us for His glory.

Every day you live and every decision you make is an investment. It's an investment in either fantasy stock or an investment in eternal stock. The books you read, the movies you watch, the friends you hang out with, the jobs you have, and the education you pursue are all investments. Which stock are you investing in?

That's what this book is about: investing in today. Living for *such a time* because *someday when* doesn't exist. Learning to live today well because today is what God has given us use for His glory, and the only alternative is a life of regrets.

Your today may already include college, a career, children, or ministry. For some of us, those are still on the way. But regardless of what your today or season looks like, it's what you and I have been given to live for God's glory. Single or married, career or college, summer or fall, today is your *such a time.*

Just like I drink smoothies in the summer and coffee in the fall, investing today is going to look different for all of us. As I have accepted this dare, living for *such a time,* I have learned many lessons. From these lessons, I'm going to tell you what I wish I had known. I think the most important lesson I learned was what it means to be "His Girl."

REFLECT

Read 1 Corinthians 7:34.

What are the *someday whens* in your life? Make a list of three:

1._____

2._____

3._____

What are some of the talents that you have been given. Make a list of at least three:

1._____

2._____

3._____

4._____

5._____

How can you start living for *such a time*, by investing what you have been given, and stop living for *someday when*?

HIS GIRL

My beloved speaks and says to me:
"Arise, my love, my beautiful one, and come away with me."
~Song of Solomon 2:10 (paraphrased)~

I wish I could tell you that learning to be "His Girl" was easy, but that's just not the case. Looking back, it is a precious memory, but this memory was forged on what felt like a brutal mountain hike. It started with an invitation. I was serving at a summer camp in California when I received the most exciting invitation in all my life:

> *Sisi, will you be my girl for the summer? Will you let me whisper your name huskily in your ear and draw you close? Will you walk with me up Lodge Hill and just be giddy about my love for you? Will you always be on the lookout for me, so you know where I am at every moment? Let me caress your hair and whisper to you. Sisi, will you be my girl?*
>
> Lord, when I think about this invitation and envision you hugging me and whispering to me, I am overwhelmed — flattered even! Talk about a fairytale

15

invitation. The God of the universe drawing close, breathing in His scent, and feeling His strong, all-powerful arms wrap around me.

As a bridegroom rejoices over his bride so God rejoices over you.

~Isaiah 62:5(b)

Samantha, as you walk through your day and creation, I want it to be as if I am leading you through my land. You are a princess from a far away land or a simple servant girl to whom I am showing my majesty. Everything I have created I designed to woo you – to prove to you my wealth, power, strength, goodness, and generosity. Together we explore it and laugh, as we plan our life together. But other moments we are just together. No planning because none is needed – we're together – enough said.

I couldn't help but respond with, "Yes Lord, I will be your girl. I will delight in all I see around me as a love letter from you, my lover. I will laugh because of your love for me. The King of Kings is in love with me! I will open up my secrets to you, knowing you will never hurt me or leave me. My heart is secure in your hands. How fun to be loved by and in love with a mighty warrior who has victory wherever He goes and is loved by His troops; who is gentle and thoughtful of others and serves beyond His assignments; who is loved by every woman and could have any He chooses. Yet I am the one who holds His heart simply by being me. Yes, Lord, I will be your girl."

Being His girl this summer meant seeking His approval and attention only. My goal was not to have every cute guy conversing with me or approval from my manager. Instead, as I walked to my job each day, I stopped to take pictures of the sky and let God's love envelope me. Walking to work everyday I learned that "His girl" is — content, intentional, and fearless.

> **"His girl" is — content, intentional, and fearless.**

Content

I used to always think of "contentment" as a synonym for "complacency." But contentment is not complacency. Contentment is trusting and embracing where God has brought you. Contentment takes courage and action. Psalm 37:3-5 says:

> *Trust in the Lord and do good; dwell in the land and enjoy safe pasture. Take delight in the Lord and He will give you the desires of your heart. Commit your way to the Lord and trust Him.*

SUCH A TIME

While I received the most exciting invitation ever in California, that's not where I had wanted to spend my summer. But God had revealed to me in multiple ways that California is where He needed me that summer. So, I boarded a plane. I won't pretend that I didn't scare my brother half to death by crying during both flights, but I went. I banked on who I knew God was — a good God who would only bring me to good places. So, in the middle-of-nowhere California, I unpacked my bags and set up camp.

I made a courageous decision to be content. Courageously, I trusted that God had brought me to a good place, which is consistent with His character, and I chose to dwell there. So often when God brings us to another pasture, we celebrate. After the celebration, we turn to Jesus, who just brought us to this lush land, expecting Him to lead us to an even greener pasture. I can't imagine how this must grieve His heart. He just brought us to the perfect place for us to grow in our individual season of life, yet we don't appreciate it.

Elisabeth Elliot put it this way in her book, *Let Me Be a Woman*:

> Single life may be only a stage of a life's journey, but even a stage is a gift. God may replace it with another gift, but the receiver accepts His gifts with thanksgiving. This gift, for this day. The life of faith is

> lived one day at a time, and it has to be lived—not always looked forward to as though the "real" living were around the next corner. It is today for which we are responsible. God still owns tomorrow.

Our courageous decision includes embracing today, which requires action. After arriving in California, I didn't leave my clothes in my suitcase. No, I unpacked them. I expected the Lord to have an amazing adventure in store for me. I invested in those around me, built relationships, and attended every meeting possible.

Psalm 37 instructs us to trust, dwell, and ENJOY. There are things in the place that God has brought you that are only in this place. Don't miss out on a single thing where God has you, *today*.

As I took action, I realized that contentment, for me, was not giving up on dreams, but rather, embracing the dreams God had for me. My dream was to choreograph a flash mob and publish a book over the summer. His dream was for me to receive an invitation, accept the invitation, and get to know who He was.

Contentment is not giving up on my dreams, but embracing the dreams God has for me.

Intentional

The better we know who God is, the better we know who He says we are and who He wants us to be. This is important because being "His Girl" means caring more about what He thinks about us than anything else.

For example, when you're "in love," all you care about is what "Prince Charming" thinks. All your energy is put into learning his likes and dislikes. Getting his attention with your actions and appearance consumes all your thoughts and energy. Some girls even go as far as changing their dreams and interests to match his!

In other words, you're intentional. You dress with intent, act with intent, speak with intent, and even dream with intent — all to receive his attention.

We desire for a certain young man to notice us and are intentional about fulfilling that desire. Psalm 37:4 says, *Take delight in the Lord and He will give you the desires of your heart.* I wonder what life would look like and who I would be if I intentionally delighted in the Lord by focusing my attention and actions to receive God's approval and affirmation.

I love the way Max Lucado depicts his character Lucia from *You Are Special*:

The Wemmicks were small wooden people. Each of the wooden people was carved by a woodworker named Eli. Each Wemmick had a box of golden star stickers and a box of gray dot stickers.

Up and down the streets all over the city, people could be seen sticking stars or dots on one another. The pretty ones, those with smooth wood and fine paint, always got stars. But if the wood was rough or the paint chipped, the Wemmicks gave dots.

Punchinello was one of these. One day he met a Wemmick who was unlike any he'd ever met. She had no dots or stars. Her name was Lucia. It wasn't that people didn't try to give her stickers; it's just that the stickers didn't stick.

Why didn't the stickers stick? That's exactly what Punchinello asked Eli, to which Eli answered:

Because she has decided that what I think is more important than what they think. The stickers only stick if you let them. The stickers only stick if they matter to you. The more you trust my love, the less you care about the stickers.

Instead of spending her day sticking stickers on other Wemmicks, Lucia found herself daily listening to Eli tell her who she was. Lucia was intentional. Everyday she climbed the hill to Eli's workshop to be with Him. She did not seek out stars of approval from the other Wemmicks; rather, she delighted herself in her Maker.

When they did give her stickers, they didn't stick because she already knew who Eli said she was. Dots did not define her. Stars did not give her value. Only what Eli said about her made a difference. She knew what He said about her and didn't care what the others said.

I want to be like Lucia. When I intentionally delight in who God is and who He says I am, I don't spend time seeking others' approval. Instead, I make decisions confidently, without fear of what others think, because I know what my Creator thinks. I am not distracted with men or ambitions, but completely focused on my heavenly bridegroom.

Fearless

Finally, "His Girl" is fearless. Aware of her heavenly bridegroom's love for her, she walks with boldness wherever He leads. Because "His Girl" has chosen to be content and embrace the place where God has her learning about Him and lives intentionally, she can know where God is calling her and walk confidently—even when it doesn't makes sense.

Frequently, God calls "His Girls" to do things that are scary, don't make sense, or aren't what you want. Esther didn't want to go to the King, yet she knew that it was what God was calling her to do. So, she obeyed, leaving her fate in God's hands even though it didn't make sense to her because she was "His Girl."

We already established that California was the last place I wanted to spend my summer. I had reasons—I wanted to stay home, pursue writing, speaking, and physical training. Staying home made sense with who I believed God wanted me to become—an author, speaker, and personal trainer, who ministered to women full-time.

Despite how unreasonable spending my entire summer in California seemed, I went because that's where my good God told me to go. He didn't give me any promises or "This is why I am sending you to California." He just said, "I love you," and "California is where I want you." And, just like the story of Esther, God came through for me.

Not only did I receive the greatest invitation of my life in California, but the Lord also clarified the ministry He wanted me to pursue. He taught me the importance of caring for myself in full-time ministry. I learned the power of prayer and cultivated a deeper relationship with Him than I could have ever imagined.

Looking back, I realize how critical my summer in California was to who God is leading me to become. What I saw as foolish and opposite of where He wanted me to go was exactly in line with the journey He has for me. But it took bravery to see what God had done.

Esther would never have saved her people if she did not proceed fearlessly to what appeared to be definite death. I would never have learned the depth of God's vision for me if I had not ventured where my heart felt fear.

Conclusion

Shortly after accepting that magnificent proposal, I wrote in my journal:

> If I am "His Girl" all I want to do is what He wants me to do; I only want to be where He wants me to be; I only want to be recognized as His; I only care what He thinks.

But this is not an invitation God extends to only me. He's extending it to you, too. Song of Solomon 2:20 says:

> *My beloved speaks and says to me: "Arise, my love, my beautiful one, and come away with me."*

Accepting is scary, but it's in daring to be **content**, unpacking our bags and setting up camp in the place God has brought us to, that we discover who God is and learn how valuable we are. **Intentionally** seeking who we are in the Lord allows us to approach every circumstance with confidence and joy because we know who we are to Him. Finally, "His Girl" steps forth **fearlessly**, not because she has no fear, but because she knows who God is and what He calls her.

It doesn't mean we won't cry in the airport on our way and scare our best friend, but His love will be stronger than our fear and we will get to see how truly good He is. And when we do, we won't feel like Rapunzel, cooped up in her tower, singing, "When will my life begin . . . ?"

REFLECT

Read Song of Solomon 2:10 and Psalm 37:3-5.

What do you feel is most important for you as "His Girl" — contentment, intentional living, or fearlessness?

What do you struggle with most as "His Girl" — contentment, intentional living, or fearlessness?

How would your life change if you accepted the invitation to be "His Girl?"

WHEN WILL MY LIFE BEGIN . . .

I will move ahead, bold and confident
Taking every step in obedience
While I'm waiting
I will serve You
While I'm waiting
I will worship
While I'm waiting
I will not faint
I'll be running the race
Even while I wait
~"While I'm Waiting" by Matt Maher~

While accepting the invitation to be "His Girl" was life-changing, I still found myself waiting around all the time. Living content, intentional, and fearless didn't erase waiting from my life. Frequently, I found myself idly brushing my hair like Rapunzel with no purpose.

Swinging my legs, I couldn't help but wonder, "When will my life begin?" After all, I was "His Girl" now. As I was soon to learn, being "His Girl" requires quite a bit of waiting. But waiting as "His Girl" doesn't mean pining away for Prince Charming; instead, it requires goals, action, and preparation.

The summer after I graduated high school was the summer I learned to wait. It was also arguably the most difficult and pivotal summer of my life. Graduating was exhilarating. The exhilaration was shortly shattered, however, when I received a letter declining my application to intern with the leadership ministry I had poured my heart and soul into throughout high school.

My dream of four years, which I had believed God had given me, was crushed by a mere piece of paper splattered with ink. For the rest of the summer I cried, endeavoring to believe that God had a better plan for my life. Then I cried some more because no matter how "patiently" I waited or hard I listened, God didn't tell me what to do. He pulled my dream out from under me and then stayed silent. Or, so I thought.

Today I can see that the problem wasn't God's silence; rather, it was my waiting. I don't know about you, but when I hear "waiting," I think of Rapunzel, singing this song from *Tangled*:

SUCH A TIME

7 am, the usual morning lineup:
Start on the chores and sweep 'til the floor's all clean
Polish and wax, do laundry, and mop and shine up
Sweep again, and by then it's like 7:15.

And so I'll read a book
Or maybe two or three
I'll add a few new paintings to my gallery
I'll play guitar and knit
And cook and basically
Just wonder when will my life begin?

Basically she's whiling away the time, or worse, being lazy as she brushes her golden river of hair for the thousandth time while waiting for Prince Charming. Rapunzel has no purpose, no direction, and does whatever will make the time pass.

Two things happen in this situation. Either you do a little of this and that, and end up feeling as though you've wasted your life, or, like me, you participate in every possible activity, hoping that it will give you value, and end up not having time for anything you truly want to do.

I can't help but wonder what would happen if I trained for my triathlon in this manner. Swimming one day, lifting weights the next, throwing in some yoga or maybe zumba . . . you know. Perhaps, I would go out to lunch with friends a couple days a week, work on writing this book, and accidentally plan a camping trip right on top of my race. All in an effort to fill the time between now and race day!

First, my method of training would be completely off. If I am going to swim, bike, and run for almost two hours, I need to train swimming, biking, and running consecutively on the same day. Second, how could I have possibly found myself camping on the very same day I was supposed to compete in my long-awaited race?!

What if, when we heard the word "wait," we thought—
goal-oriented?

By definition, "wait" means to rest in expectation; to be in attendance to; to continue by reason of hindrance (*Webster*, 1828). An athlete trains in expectation of a race. Ladies-in-waiting frequently wait to fulfill the bidding of their mistress. If you are stuck in a traffic jam on your way to work, you are still on your way to work, regardless of the hindrance.

Each of these definitions includes a specific destination. If there is a destination, then there is a goal. Therefore, waiting implies that there is a goal.

Your goal determines your form of waiting. If my goal is to run a triathlon, I will wait for my race differently than if I am waiting for my date to arrive and take me to dinner. Either I will train to properly prepare for the race, or I will try on three outfits to find just the right one in expectation of my special evening.

When I sign up for a race, I sign up with the training in mind. To be honest, that's the whole reason I pay to swim, bike, and run for almost two hours. Race day is my incentive to train during the time of expectation.

It's the same with going out. Part of the fun of having a dance is getting dressed up for the event. The waiting, expectation, and preparation are part of the moment. The goal makes the waiting fun.

Unfortunately, in life we rarely have a specific date for which we are waiting. That's what makes waiting difficult—The not knowing. We don't have to have all the reasons and answers. But we do need to have an end goal: to glorify God. Just as when I trained for my triathlon, I asked myself, "What do I need to do to be able to race," I ask God, "What do I need to do to glorify you?"

If glorifying God is my goal, I need to know what glorifies Him. In the story at the beginning of this chapter, I shared how I waited for God to tell me what to do. What I didn't tell you was that while I waited, I didn't do anything! I was so afraid that I might accidentally do something God didn't want me to do that I didn't do anything.

Mark Batterson put it this way in his book, *In a Pit with a Lion on a Snowy Day:*

> Some of us act like faithfulness is making no turnovers when faithfulness is actually scoring touchdowns. (119)

Waiting isn't avoiding the ball like the plague because, if we have possession, there's a possibility we will fumble. That would be like me signing up for the triathlon and never training because the water might be too cold to swim in or because I might not come in first.

Waiting is doing everything we can to catch the ball when God throws it to us—because we *might* make a touchdown. In other words, it's me signing up for the race and training my guts out because I want to complete said triathlon!

Ultimately, waiting is doing the part God asks you to do to the best of your ability and watching God be God— whether that's scoring a touchdown, completing a triathlon, mastering a triple pirouette, or publishing a novel.

My idle waiting was wrong. God had given me a goal to glorify Him, a dream to have a ministry, and a brain to make good decisions. He also gave me wise parents who delivered an unforgettable two-hour lecture to me during which I cried almost the entire 120 minutes.

They encouraged me to take action and embrace the opportunities in my life that would develop valuable skills. Hindsight being 20/20, I can now see that is exactly what brought God glory, but, in the moment, it felt as though I were putting things in God's mouth about what He wanted me to do. . But I think that's just it.

For me, the first step to glorifying God is taking action. During said two-hour conversation, my Dad reminded me, like he had countless times before, "God can't steer a parked car. If you are parked, it doesn't matter which way He turns the wheel, you're still not going anywhere. You have to at least be in motion, so God can direct you."

When I listened to my parents and got in motion by taking advantage of the opportunities that had come, I found that they were doors that the Lord had opened in my life. It was His way of saying, "Samantha, this is what I want you to do. This is the way you will glorify me."

But it wasn't until I walked through the doors that He had opened that I realized He was the one who had opened them. James says, "Show me your faith without deeds and I will show you my faith by what I do" (James 2:18).

When I waited doing nothing, I was suffering from what I call "Rapunzel Paralysis." Instead of embracing the opportunities that the Lord had given me, I was wondering when my life would begin. We can wait and wonder, like Rapunzel, "When will my life begin . . . ?" or we can wait with expectation, declaring, "Today, my life has begun!"

Just like training for my triathlon required me to realize that the race started the day I registered, we need to live life as though it *has* begun. God has given us a goal to glorify Him, brains to make good decisions, and opportunities to choose from. It's time we realize that life has begun and try to score some touchdowns, maybe even complete a triathlon! Enough of brushing your golden hair while you're "waiting."

God can't steer a parked car. We need to do our part and trust that God will do His, no matter how long He asks us to wait.

Waiting Well

If we got to ask God "Why?" when He has us in a season of waiting, I wonder what He would say. I think Elisabeth Elliot has a good guess in *Passion and Purity*:

> I *realized* that the deepest spiritual lessons are not learned by His letting us have our way in the end, but

> by His making us wait, bearing with us in love and patience until we are able to honestly pray what He taught His disciples to pray: Thy will be done.

Waiting, like everything else in life, has nothing to do with us and everything to do with God. Bringing God glory, making us into His likeness, being ready for His plan for our life—it comes down to stewarding waiting well. In the parable of the ten virgins, five wait well and are rewarded:

> At that time the kingdom of heaven will be like ten virgins who took their lamps and went out to meet the bridegroom. Five of them were foolish and five were wise. The foolish ones took their lamps but did not take any oil with them. The wise ones, however, took oil in jars along with their lamps. The bridegroom was a long time in coming, and they all became drowsy and fell asleep.
>
> At midnight the cry rang out: "Here's the bridegroom! Come out to meet him!"
>
> Then all the virgins woke up and trimmed their lamps. 8 The foolish ones said to the wise, "Give us some of your oil; our lamps are going out."
>
> "No," they replied, "there may not be enough for both us and you. Instead, go to those who sell oil and buy some for yourselves."

SUCH A TIME

> But while they were on their way to buy the oil, the bridegroom arrived. The virgins who were ready went in with him to the wedding banquet. And the door was shut.
>
> Later the others also came. "Lord, Lord," they said, "open the door for us!"
>
> But he replied, "Truly I tell you, I don't know you."
>
> Therefore keep watch, because you do not know the day or the hour. (Matthew 25:1–13)

Both the wise women and the foolish women had a goal they were waiting for—the bridegroom's arrival. The wise women filled their lamps, brought along extra oil, and remained alert even though they had no idea when the bridegroom would arrive.

The foolish women, convinced that the bridegroom would arrive shortly, only brought their lamps—no extra oil. They even fell asleep while they waited. Later, while the five who were prepared celebrated, the foolish women were not allowed to join the wedding feast because they were not prepared.

The virgins did not get to choose the time and manner in which the bridegroom arrived. They were simply required to wait. Later, they were rewarded according to the way they waited. It's the same with us. We don't get to choose the timing and way God will show up and write our lives. But we do get to choose the way we will wait.

I for one am determined to wait well, like the five wise virgins. I will be prepared. Just like the virgins' ability to attend the feast depended on their waiting, my ability to fulfill the will of God depends on the way I wait. I'm not going to miss any feast that the Lord might have scheduled for my life, even if it's a snack in the middle of the night. I choose to wait well and be prepared!

***

Pretend I'm your big sister for a moment or that dancer in the sparkly tutu you always wanted to be just like because I have something I want to tell you. Here it is — "There is no end to waiting."

I used to think that someday I would be on the other side of this season of "waiting." But no sooner do I finish waiting for one thing, than I'm waiting for another. There are moments of waiting every day, and there are opportunities I wait for day after day. I've begun to wonder, "If I'm always going to be waiting, what's the point of waiting for waiting to end?"

So, from now on, I'm going to wait as if I'm waiting in line at a bank. While I wait, I am confident that I will be helped, even if I do have to wait for an hour! There's no way I'm getting out of line. When it's finally my turn, I will be prepared because while I was in line, I completed all the paperwork and found my debit card.

Psalms 27:14 says, "Wait for the Lord, be strong and take heart; and wait for the Lord." Waiting is so much more than I ever thought it was. That excruciating summer after high school taught me that waiting is not for the weak or faint of heart. Rather, waiting is for the strong of heart and determined in spirit.

It's not easy; in fact, I'll be the first to admit that I hate waiting. But God promises that those who wait will be strengthened, soar on wings like eagles, and have a good inheritance. It's as though if we choose to wait well for the glory of God—with a goal in mind—instead of whiling away the time like Rapunzel, God is ensuring us a touchdown, a better opportunity than said internship, and a successful triathlon, as well as a seat at the wedding feast.

Holding Pattern

Staring out the window at the tiny airport and city below, my friend could barely contain her excitement. After flying for a total of 14 hours, she was finally about to set her foot in Indonesia where she would finally be a mission's nurse. Gradually, she realized that the plane was flying in circles. Frustrated she looked out the window again. There below her was the airport.

Stopping a flight attendant she asked, "Why aren't we landing? I can see the airport."

"We are in a holding pattern," the flight attendant replied.

"What is a 'holding pattern'?"

"A 'holding pattern' is when the plane flies in a circle, hovering over the airport, until there is space to land."

"Oh," my friend looked out the window again.

Reading my friend's unasked question, the flight attendant assured her, "The captain said we are second in line to land, so it shouldn't be much longer."

Smiling her thanks, my friend watched the flight attendant walk down the long hallway illuminated by lights lining the narrow path to where she took her seat and buckled, preparing for landing.

I love this story. It reminds me of how I often see life while convincing me of how I *should* see my life. So often I feel as though I am in an endless sea of pointless waiting. Just like my friend, I cannot see the long line of planes that are making immediate landing unsafe.

But my Pilot can.

This story challenges me to see waiting as tenacious — holding fast, persevering, and determined. This tenacious waiting requires goals, expectation, and action. Waiting well, having goals, taking action, and preparing are awesome, but the best part is when connecting the dots reveals a picture!

REFLECT

Read Isaiah 40:30–31 and Psalms 27:14.

What are three things you are waiting for?

1._____

2._____

3._____

How are you waiting—like Rapunzel or the wise maidens?

Waiting is goal-oriented. What is the goal you are waiting for?

How do you need to change your waiting in orientation to your goal?

CONNECTING THE DOTS

Whatever you do, work at it with all your heart,
as working for the Lord, not for human masters.
~Colossians 3:23~

Every summer I reevaluate my schedule, what I am currently doing, where I want to go in life, and what I need to do to get there. Summer skips in with sunny days spent with my siblings, but there are still those occasional stormy days that have me feeling lost. Lost as a pencil on a blank piece of paper trying to find the next dot.

Do you remember those connect-the-dots pictures you used to do in coloring books when you were young? That's what this season feels like—connecting dots. All I know is that the picture that will emerge from this blank piece of paper speckled with dots will glorify God.

It's the not knowing what those black dots are and how to get to the next one that leaves me feeling lost. I so badly want to do what God wants me to do and to do it His way. And there are so many opportunities in my life,

I get overwhelmed. I don't know which one is the dot God placed on my piece of paper to create the picture He envisions.

My senior year in high school was pivotal to my learning how to connect the dots in my life. Several of my friends from the worship dance ministry I was a part of were auditioning to work at Busch Gardens as dancers. In the car on our way out of the neighborhood one day, I proposed, "Mom, I really want to audition to work at Busch Gardens as a dancer. Would you please consider and talk to Dad about whether or not I am allowed?"

She was silent for a while. Then she answered, "Yes, I will talk to your father, but why do you want to work for Busch Gardens?"

"I would be getting paid to dance. What could be better than that? I would be a professional dancer—a dream come true!"

"Yes, I can see how that would be fun," she responded thoughtfully, "but what skills will you be developing? What goal would dancing at Busch Gardens help you reach?"

"Ummm, I would be learning different types of dance and interacting with other dancers. I would also be making a dream come true since getting paid to dance would make me a semi-professional dancer."

"Uh-hum."

Again, my mother nodded and stayed quiet long enough for me to begin to feel uncomfortable. Peeking over, I could see she was thinking, but I wanted her to say something. When I finally had given up and was about to change the subject, she voiced, "Samantha, it's not that I don't want you to have fun or get paid to do something that you love, but I think the most important question is: Will being a dancer at Busch Gardens develop skills that will help you get to where you believe God wants you to be?"

That was all I needed to hear. That was all I needed to ask myself. And, it continues to be all I need to ask myself when trying to find the next dot on my blank piece of paper.

> **Will being a dancer at Busch Gardens**
> **develop skills that will help you get**
> **to where you believe God wants you to be?**

Intentional

The most significant part to connecting your dots in life is being intentional. Which dot are you going to next? Why? Where will that dot take you? Which dot will you be closer to by going to the one you've chosen?

In the case of auditioning to be a dancer at Busch Gardens, I asked myself, "How will being a dancer at

Busch Gardens develop skills that will get me to where I believe God wants me to be?"

Before answering this question, I needed to define what I believed God wanted me to do with my life long-term. As a woman, I believed that God had called me to someday be a wife and mom, supporting my husband and raising children. As an individual, God had put the desire in my heart to go into full-time women's ministry, writing, speaking, and hosting conferences.

After identifying my long-term goal, I rephrased the question, "How will being a dancer at Busch Gardens help me become a writer or public speaker in women's ministry?"

This question led me to create a list of the skills I could potentially gain from dancing at Busch Gardens: increased dance skills, larger knowledge of choreography, relationships with other dancers, better stage presence. Although all those are good areas to grow in, none of them were dots I needed to connect to complete the picture I believed God was creating with my life.

Finding the Dots

I realize that being intentional may have been simpler for me than it will be for you. Neither of my sisters had as clear a destination as I did. They both want to be wives and mothers. The question was what should they do until then. As we sought the Lord, we thought about what they enjoyed doing and were good at. God gives us gifts to use for His glory. 1 Peter 4:10–11 says:

> Each of you should use whatever gift you have received to serve others, as faithful stewards of God's grace in its various forms.
>
> *If* anyone speaks, they should do so as one who speaks the very words of God. If anyone serves, they should do so with the strength God provides, so that in all things God may be praised through Jesus Christ. To him be the glory and the power for ever and ever.

And Romans 12:4–8 encourages us:

> For just as each of us has one body with many members, and these members do not all have the same function, 5 so in Christ we, though many, form one body, and each member belongs to all the others. 6 We have different gifts, according to the grace given to each of us.
>
> If your gift is prophesying, then prophesy in accordance with your faith; 7 if it is serving, then serve; if it is teaching, then teach; 8 if it is to encourage, then give encouragement; if it is giving, then give generously; if it is to lead, do it diligently; if it is to show mercy, do it cheerfully.

We knew that God had given my sisters strengths that would bring Him glory. So, we prayed and pondered, "What do they enjoy doing and feel like they are good at?" Gradually, the Lord revealed to us that my sister Rachel felt called to over sea missions while Beth loved graphic design, photography, and building websites.

Once we discovered what my sisters enjoyed doing, we asked, "What education does Rachel need to be a missionary in Africa? What skill does Beth need to develop to be a web designer, blogger, and photographer?" From there, we were able to begin connecting dots.

Currently, Beth is taking classes in web design, and photography. She is also teaching herself how to read HTML. And, Rachel, at the time of writing this chapter, just got accepted into the local nursing program!

Completed Picture

My sisters and I don't have a completed picture or know what the finished picture will be. But we do know that it will be a masterpiece that will glorify God. So, dot by dot, class time or free time, we intentionally seek to glorify Him. And, dot by dot, we get closer to completing the picture. The most exciting part is, that one day far from now, we'll look back and all those stormy summer days when we felt lost in vast blankness will be worth it—more than worth it.

While the end picture is more than worth it, it's easy to get distracted. When I get distracted, even by good things, I begin putting my value into what I do instead of whose I am. When the expectation to connect the dots in our lives becomes more important than being "His Girl," it doesn't matter how many dots we connect, the picture will never be beautiful enough. As you seek to be "His Girl," connect your dots, and live your "such a time," it's important to know what the expectations are.

REFLECT

Read Colossians 3:23.

What are three "dots" in your life right now?

1._____

2._____

3._____

What do you believe God wants you to do with your life?

Ask yourself: "How will _____ (insert "dot") get me closer to being _____ (what God wants you to be/do)?

SUCH AN EXPECTATION

This is my son, whom I love and am well pleased with.
~Matthew 3:17~

Somewhere between figuring out this whole life-after-high-school thing, being "His Girl, and waiting well, I started to believe that connecting all the dots in my life was the most important thing. The more dots I connected and the more magnificent their connection, the more valuable I was.

Going back to that summer in California, I learned that these expectations were wrong. Instead, the only expectation I needed to live up to was simple—be me. This lesson came in the form of a tree.

Sitting on a stump and leaning back against a great oak, I surveyed the little clearing I had found to spend the next twenty-four hours seeking the Creator of my crude wooden throne. I sighed. The last fourteen days had been rough—so rough, in fact, I was beginning to wonder who I was.

All of my fellow staff related with each other based on what college they were attending, which degree they were pursuing, who they were "with," and which sorority or fraternity they were a part of. When any of them asked me about where I went to school and I replied, "I don't. Actually, I run two dance ministries, am the office manager for my father's business, coordinate a statewide leadership program, and am a professional harpist," they politely listened, but it didn't mean anything to them. All they heard was that I didn't go to college. While I was well-known throughout my community at my home in Virginia, I had little to no identity in this place.

With swirling thoughts, I drew my knees up to my chest. I stared at an imposing tree directly across from me. Somehow it seemed to know exactly who it was. How could a vertical log with green fringe for hair know who it was when I didn't?

"Why don't I know who I am?" I murmured as my eyes traveled up its trunk to the leaves, which let diamonds of sunlight through to scatter on the ground. That's when I heard it. It wasn't a bird chirping or the wind whistling, but a still, small voice, inaudible, and yet so real.

> *Samantha, you need to be like these trees. They stand tall and strong and immovable. They wear the bark I have given them, no matter the season or circumstances. They do not wish to be*

somewhere else but are content where I have placed them. They bear fruit, drop seeds, grow and change colors without compromising or trying to be like the other trees. They simply are what I made them to be, and do what I made them to do.

What if the pine decided to be like the other trees and wanted to lose its needles? Or an apple tree wanted to grow acorns instead of apples?

These trees stand tall, defying all odds and proclaiming me, simply because all they know is what I created them to be. They cannot talk like you, walk like you, or think like you. And yet they never cease to bring me glory.

Glorifying me and making me known isn't done through doing and serving, dancing and speaking, or even being the most righteous. I am glorified most when you simply are who I made you to be. When you are aware and confident of who you are because of me and who I am in you, I will be glorified.

Finally, lifting my pen from my journal, these words echoed in my mind — *They cannot talk like you, walk like you, or think like you. And yet they never cease to bring me glory . . . I am most glorified when you simply are who I made you to be.*

Simply His

That caused me to wonder, "Who did God make me to be?"

Ephesians 5:1-2 instructs us to be imitators of Christ. One of my favorite lessons about Jesus concerns His baptism. When the dove descended on Him and the heavenly voice resounded, "This is my son whom I love and am well pleased with" (Matthew 3:17), Jesus had yet to do a single miracle.

Even though Jesus had done nothing, He was loved by His father and made His father proud. Jesus had simply been who His father created Him to be—His son. Just as the trees bring God glory by being trees, Jesus brought His father glory by being a human. In the same way, I bring glory to God just by being His daughter.

Suddenly, I realized that it was my expectations that were confusing me and making me feel identity-less. It wasn't the trees or my co-workers questions stripping my value. It was my expectations—my expectations that didn't line up with God's expectations for me.

I thought bringing Him glory meant being the best at everything I did, never saying "no" to someone who needed help, running two ministries, loving my siblings, and working two jobs. But God had asked me to be His, plain and simple. No miracles, no crown, no degree—just His Girl.

The weight of this realization knocked the wind out of me. I looked up to the sky and cried. I sobbed because I realized that my life and mind were like a beehive swarming with expectations that I could never fulfill.

That's when I stopped. I turned my journal to a clean page and began to write. Pages later I had a list of all the self-expectations I could possibly think of. This is a very abbreviated list:

- Never say no
- Dress perfectly, modestly, and fashionably
- Always set a flawless example of Christ
- Never cry
- Never yell at my siblings
- Read the Bible every day for an hour
- Be independent in working for my Dad even though I don't know what to do
- Come to Mom's rescue at all hours
- Exercise 5 days a week, hard enough that I'm sore that next day
- Never be tired, always have enough sleep
- Eat perfectly healthy and never cheat or treat
- Be productive, always have results

God's Expectations

Writing this list led me to wonder, "What are God's expectations for me? What would life be like if the expectations I have for myself are the expectation God has for me?"

In Matthew, chapter 22, a Pharisee asked Jesus, "Which is the greatest Commandment in the Law?" Essentially, the Pharisee was asking Jesus the most important thing to do. What is the number one expectation God has for us? And Jesus replied:

> "Love the Lord your God with all your heart and with all your soul and with all your mind." This is the first and greatest commandment.
>
> ~Matthew 22:34–38

The tree loved God by being what God made it to be — a tree! Not only that, but the tree was the type of tree God designed it to be. Jesus loved God by being a human, a perfect, sinless, obedient human.

I love God by being "His Girl." When I choose to be who He created me to be, I am admitting that I am valuable just the way He made me. I am admitting that running a ministry is not what gives me value. I am admitting that making it into the college of my dreams is not what gives me identity.

New Identity

As I transitioned my identity from my "doing" to "being," I found that being who God said I am was so simple that it was complicated. Everything in me craved to be real, thirsted to be valuable, and desired to have identity.

When God gave me the picture of the tree, He challenged everything I had built my identity on. He was no longer content with me finding my identity in serving Him and bringing Him glory. *He* wanted to be my identity.

God wants to be your identity, too.

I learned that being "His Girl" is choosing His identity over my own; after all, I was made in His image (Genesis 1). Galatians 2:20 says that, as a new creation, we no longer live, but Christ lives in us. Learning how to just be who He created me to be took me on a journey of getting to know who I am in Him because if He lives in me, I now bear His identity. So I made a list of all the things He is. Here are a few:

- God is the Prince of Peace.
- God is strong.
- God is victorious.
- God is a good communicator.
- God is not afraid.
- God is beautiful.
- God is in control.

When I had my list of everything that God was, I rewrote them, including what they made me:

- God is the Prince of Peace; therefore, in Him I am the princess of peace.
- God is strong; therefore, in Him I am strong.
- God is victorious; therefore, in Him I am a conqueror and have victory.
- God is a good communicator; therefore in Him I am a good communicator.
- God is not afraid; therefore, in Him I do not have to be afraid.
- God is beautiful; therefore, in Him I am beautiful.
- God is in control; therefore, in Him I am not out of control.

Choosing His identity over my own is a resolution I feel I renew multiple times a day. But every time I choose His identity, I feel more real, more valuable, and more identifiable. I realize that's what I was created for all along—not to build my own identity, but rather to walk in someone else's, someone who is much greater, more faithful, and more perfect than I ever could be.

There's a reason you and I feel miserable when we stare into our reflection of unfulfilled expectations. You and I were never created to fulfill those expectations. I wrote it this way in my journal:

> *Samantha, all the expectations you are trying to fill are your own. The only expectations you need to be concerned with are mine. And the only expectation I have for you is being the "you" I made you to be — just like the trees I created. You are special because you are mine.*

When who you are is wrapped up in what you do and what others expect you to do, you will never have an identity. That's why those trees glorified Him most. As long as they were accomplishing God's will, all was well.

When I try to fulfill my list of expectations, I feel like a wax figurine because it's me trying to be someone else or trying to fit into the outline of another person. The only outline the trees follow is God's. That's why I feel real on the days I walk in God's identity.

Just like the trees, I was created to fulfill His expectations of me and no one else's. You weren't created to be the same as Scarlett Johanson or Kate Middleton.

It's okay to be broken and not know how to connect the dots, but let's not mend our brokenness by trying to fit into another broken pot or following the advice of an incomplete picture, especially when the creator of pots and connector of dots is waiting to put us back together and drawing the lines for us more beautifully than we could ever imagine.

> *Oh Lord, teach my heart to desire only the expectations you have of me and not be burdened by the expectations of others, the world, and myself. Remind me that fulfilling others' expectations is just like being a brilliant maple and trying to grow pinecones and not lose my leaves.*
>
> *It's a silly mess of me trying to fit into the mold of someone else, who is just as empty and broken as me. But when I walk in your identity, I feel real because that's who you made me to be – your girl. When I walk in your identity, I am free to live for "such a time" because you are the one who created me for "such a time" and put me in **this** "such a time."*

Be you. Like the tree was a tree, be you. After all, that's who God created to be His friend — YOU. And the more you get to know Him as your friend, the more you will understand His expectations for you, and only HIS expectations will matter to you.

Journaling is one of my favorite ways to spend time with Him. It is also a critical tool to take your relationship with Jesus to the next level while seeking to live for *such a time*.

REFLECT

Make a list of at least 10 expectations you have for yourself or others have for you.

Make of list of at least 10 things that God is.

Pick your 3 favorite things that God is and write:

I am _____ because God is _____

SUCH A FRIEND

Cultivating my relationship with Jesus
Christ was my "such a time."
~Samantha Roose~

Just like fall is my favorite season, journaling and being friends with God is my favorite part of living my *such a time*. Waking up in the morning and sitting down with my steaming cup of coffee to read my Bible and write my thoughts in a letter format to my best friend is the highlight of my day.

This early morning habit is the power to living my *such a time* because, let's face it, it's not always easy to make the right decisions. Frequently, the right decision in my life has been letting go of things that I loved. As I have sought the Lord, He has strengthened my heart to run faithfully and see clearly His expectations for me.

Today, I can honestly say that Jesus is my best friend. But it wasn't always that way. Neither did it happen overnight. Rather, it happened when I was begging God to give me a friend.

Needing A Friend

My family had just returned from the states after a five-year tour in Germany with the United State Army. My sisters seemed to hit it off immediately with people their own age. But after living in Williamsburg for a whole year, I still didn't feel like I had any friends. Once when I complained to Mom about my friendless state, she responded, "Samantha, what if God wants to be your friend before He gives you a friend?"

Needless to say, that was not what I wanted to hear! However, it was what I needed. I rebelled against the idea for several months, waiting for *someday when* I would have a BFF. Finally, out of desperation, I decided to become God's friend.

I realized that my *such a time* in that season was to become God's friend, just like Mommy suggested. Even more than that, I realized that as long as I waited for *someday when* I had friends, I would miss out on my *such a time* today and tomorrow and the next day.

So I began to make time with the Lord a daily activity. If I missed spending time with Him in the morning, I would squeeze it in before I crawled into bed. About a year later, I vividly remember riding in our big, green fifteen-passenger van on my way home from dance practice. I felt like Thomas Edison when his one thousand and first light bulb worked! Overwhelmed, I turned to my mom and declared, "I just realized that I have had two friends for several months." Mom just smiled.

Looking back, I realize that my relationship with the Lord became so real that I no longer craved friendships with others. When I finally realized that the Lord had brought not one, but two friends, Alice and Zipporah, into my life, they were beautiful blessings, but they were not a need. God was meeting my need. My friends were fulfilling a desire, just like icing on a cake!

My Best Friend

Eighteenth century preacher and philosopher Jonathan Edwards' description of his wife-to-be, Sarah Edwards, gives us a beautiful example of what it looks like when Jesus is our best friend.

> They say there is a young lady in [New Haven] who is beloved of that Great Being, who made and rules the world, and that there are certain seasons in which this Great Being, in some way other or invisible, comes to her and fills her mind with exceeding sweet delight, and that she hardly cares for anything, except to meditate on him—that she expects after a while to be received up where he is, to be raised up out of the world and caught up into heaven; being assured that he loves her too well to let her remain at a distance from him always. There she is to dwell with him, and to be

ravished with his love and delight forever. Therefore, if you present all the world before her, with the richest of its treasures, she disregards it and cares not for it, and is unmindful of any pain or affliction. She has a strange sweetness in her mind, and singular purity in her affections; is most just and conscientious in all her conduct; and you could not persuade her to do anything wrong or sinful, if you would give her all the world, lest she should offend this Great Being. She is of a wonderful sweetness, calmness and universal benevolence of mind; especially after this Great God has manifested himself to her mind. She will sometimes go about from place to place, singing sweetly; and seems to be always full of joy and pleasure; and no one knows for what. She loves to be alone, walking in the fields and groves, and seems to have someone invisible always conversing with her. (E. D. Dodds, *Marriage to a Difficult Man* (Philadelphia: Westminster, 1971), 15)

Like Sarah Edwards, I also cherish spending time alone with my Creator. In the same way that I prefer to have conversations with my friends while walking in the woods or in a secluded booth at Starbucks, seeking God in private refreshes me. Occasionally when I find an hour free, I'll eagerly slip out of the house to wander in the woods, meditating on my God, marveling over His creation, or murmuring my thoughts to Him. I treasure these walks. There's something special about encountering God in the work of His hands.

Early in the morning, as I crawl out of my bed at six, it's not uncommon for me to groan and entertain thoughts of snuggling back under my covers (in fact, yesterday I did just that . . .). Waking before the rest of my siblings is a challenge, but worth the sacrifice. Gradually, my favorite time of the day has become these precious moments of quiet stillness accompanied by an aromatic cup of coffee, my Bible, and my journal.

During my "Jesus Time," I love to read His word and meditate on it. While I have found journaling to be the most powerful way to build my relationship with God, it wouldn't be nearly as productive without being accompanied by His letter to me. Journaling is like writing letters to God. So, it only makes sense to read His response to us — the Bible.

Typically, there are three parts to my journaling time: reading His letter, processing His letter, and writing a letter to Him. I don't always follow that order. Sometimes I'll write the letter first, then find verses that correspond with my struggle or victory, and finally rewrite the verses in my journal.

Examples

On July 14, 2014, I had a special time with the Lord that I would like to share with you:

July 14, 2014   Soaring

SUCH A TIME

After reading Isaiah 40, I copied my favorite verses down:

> He gives strength to the weary
> and increases the power of the weak.
> Even youths grow tired and weary,
> and young men stumble and fall;
> but those who hope in the LORD
> will renew their strength.
> They will soar on wings like eagles;
> they will run and not grow weary,
> they will walk and not be faint.
>
> ~Isaiah 40:29–31~

Next, I processed what meant the most to me and wrote it down:

Eagles actually fly above the altitude that birds generally fly. When eagles fly higher, they are able to catch wind currents and soar. They are not flapping their wings to fly; they are simply gliding.

Then I asked God, "What do you want me to take away from these verses?" Sitting quietly, I listened and wrote what I thought He wanted me to learn:

Samantha, I have called you to fly above your circumstances and glide in my strength and joy. You are tired. Sac-run feels impossible, scary even. You are not a night person. You are an introvert, not an extrovert. Those are your circumstances.

But I am bigger and higher than your circumstances. I am peace. I am joy. I am endurance. I am love. I am graciousness. I am strength. I am energy. I am your wind current. It is not circumstances I am calling you through. It is me I am calling you to. Soar, Samantha, soar.

Finally, I praised Him and expressed how I was going to change:

God, you are the one who makes me strong, joyful, and excited. I choose to focus on you. I will not focus on how I feel and what I see. Instead, I will focus on who I am in you.

My other favorite way to meditate on God's letter to me is to rewrite portions in my own words.

Ephesians 1:3–8 says:

Praise be to the God and Father of our Lord Jesus Christ, who has blessed us in the heavenly realms with every spiritual blessing in Christ. For he chose us in him before the creation of the world to be holy and blameless in his sight.

In love he predestined us for adoption to sonship through Jesus Christ, in accordance with his pleasure and will— to the praise of his glorious grace, which he has freely given us in the One he loves. In him we have redemption through his blood, the forgiveness of sins, in accordance with the riches of God's grace that he lavished on us.

I personalized it to say:

Praise be to my God and Father of my Lord Jesus Christ, who has blessed me in the heavenly realms with every spiritual blessing in Christ—I am lacking nothing. Even among the angels, I am considered blessed. He chose me in him before the creation of the world to be holy, perfect, and blemishless in his sight.

In love, he wanted me and desired to adopt me through Jesus Christ. It was His greatest will and pleasure to make me His own. In him I am redeemed through his blood, my sins are forgiven, and He overwhelms me with the riches of God's grace.

Since that "light bulb" moment on Ironbound Road contemplating the oak, my relationship with the Lord has continued to grow like a tree. But this beautiful growth began with death.

Death that Gives Life

Just like an acorn, which dreams of becoming a mighty oak, must first be fractured, my dream of having a best friend had to splinter. When an acorn breaks, it is awakened to a new dream—an enduring dream—a dream of growing roots which will serve as a secret support system and nutrient provider without which a giant oak would never survive to leave acorns of its own. Similarly, when my dream for a human friend died, I stopped living for *someday when*, and was awakened to a new dream of being friends with my Creator, the King of Kings, and Savior of the world. Cultivating my relationship with Jesus Christ was my *such a time*.

My relationship with my heavenly Father allows me to enjoy friendships, pour into others, and know who I am—His Girl. As my relationship with God strengthened and my roots in His word deepened, my branches have stretched farther than an acorn could ever dream. The *someday-when*-I-have-a-friend dream now seems silly.

Daily my relationship with God refreshes me and satisfies my soul more than any friendship ever could. And I have found that the friendships I have today far surpass all of my previous dreams. In fact, they are richer and more encouraging.

The Lord has produced fruit in my life through friendships, opportunities, and struggles that I could never have experienced if my dream for a "best friend" had not first shattered. In deserting *someday when* and becoming His friend, I experienced the *such a time* God had for me. Little did I know that becoming His friend would mean becoming best friends with my siblings as well . . .

REFLECT

Read Ephesians 1:3–8.

Rewrite Ephesians 1:3–8 in your own words.

Schedule a one hour "date" with Jesus this week. Make yourself a cup of coffee, or curl up in a booth at Panera with a steaming cup of chai. Read the book of Ruth and journal what you learned.

SUCH A SIBLING

Friends love at all times and a brother is born for adversity.
~Proverbs 17:17~

In the beginning, being best friends with my siblings was my least favorite part of living for *such a time*. Today, my Instagram will prove that my siblings are a highlight of my *such a time*. Desperately trying to be a good big sister, I searched high and low for resources, inspiration, and how-tos, anything to help me build a good relationship with my siblings. And guess how much I found . . . nothing!

Because my siblings have played such a vital and precious role in my *such a time*, I'm going to share with you the pain, beauty, and practical points I encountered in my journey of learning how to be best friends with my siblings. Before you begin, let me be the first to warn you, it's didn't start out pretty.

SUCH A TIME

> "I LOVE YOU!" I yelled at my 8-year-old brother from across the dining room.
>
> "No, you don't," he spat out with equal fury, "You hate me."

Before that day I always thought the phrase "her blood was boiling" was only a description used in books, but ....

Blood boiling, I stomped out of the room like an erupting volcano. I couldn't remember when it happened or how it happened. All I knew was that he was right. I hated my brother with a white-hot hatred. Being in the same room with him was like turning a pot of water on high, only I reached 212 degrees three times as fast.

My parents told me that I needed to respect my brother and love him, but all I could do was rehash my mile-long list of how he wouldn't obey me, refused to respect me, always stepped on my toes, and infuriated me by just looking at me. As far as I was concerned, I was giving him exactly what he deserved. *Someday when* he decided to respect me and treat me like a lady, then I would respect him in return. However, somewhere deep in my heart, I knew my parents were right.

I even remember asking God to change my heart and help me love my brother, but day after day my blood

69

would boil much faster than that pot of water. I don't know exactly what I expected the Lord to do—immediately erase the hatred in my heart for my brother, maybe, and replace it with warm fuzzies? However, I do know that did not happen. Not matter how much I prayed, I still hated him just as much as before!

Eventually, the Lord showed me that my brother was not the only one I was hurting. My hatred and bitterness were hurting my whole family. And, ultimately, I was hurting myself.

It's A God Thing

Proverbs 17:17 says, "A friend loves at all times, but a brother is born for adversity." At this season of my life, I wished this verse translated to, "Friends make life easy and enjoyable while brothers and sisters make life extremely difficult and unbearable."

Unfortunately, that's not what this verse means at all. What God taught me through this verse is exactly what my parents have told me since before I can remember, "Friends will come and go, but you can't get rid of your siblings." While my friends may love me deeply, it's my brothers and sisters who will be my siblings no matter what.

God specifically selected my brothers and sisters to be intimately tied to my life through thick and thin. The brother who made my blood boil is included in that list of siblings. But there's an even more exciting and more convicting part. The exciting part is that God chose me to be his big sister. The convicting part is that in choosing me to be his big sister, God gave me the responsibility to encourage him and set an example of a godly woman. My brother was not thrown into my life, neither was I thrown into his. Instead, we were put into the same family for *such a time*.

When the Lord opened my eyes to the influence and responsibility He had given me in my brother's life, I was overwhelmed. Gradually it hit me that someday my brother will be a man who will lead a family and make a difference in his community as a businessman, pastor, or maybe even president.

As my brother's older sister, God had given me the privilege of contributing to the man God has called him to be and setting an example for the woman that he will one day marry. Making me his sister, God has given me the opportunity to invest in who he becomes and those he impacts. Little did I know that as I abandoned my *someday-when*-he-respects-me-I'll-respect-him   mentality and embraced the fact that I was his sister for *such a time*, that our relationship would transform into one of my most important friendships.

Getting Practical

The first thing I had to do to restore my relationship with my brother was apologize. Blood boiling, from humiliation this time, I swallowed my mountainous pride and sat down on my brother's floor, strewn with Legos and blankets.

"Ben," I took a huge breath and held it, "I'm sorry for the way I have been treating you, saying negative things to you and being mean. That was wrong. I have not been the sister to you that God called me to be. Will you please forgive me?"

I guess I thought that after apologizing and being forgiven, our relationship would magically be restored. But that's not what happened. Not even remotely! To my horrified surprise, I apologized at least another three times before I began to see a minute change.

During this time, I began researching ways to build a good relationship with my brother. I watched videos, read books, and searched the Bible. The only answer I found was to honor your brother and respect your brother. But that's not what I was looking for. I already knew I needed to honor and respect my brother.

What I wanted to know were the practical ways to honor and respect my brother. What I am about to share with you are not answers I found in books or online; rather, they are answers that I found through trial and error while earnestly seeking the Lord.

1. **Set the example.** In my relationships with my brother I wanted him to change before I changed. 1 Timothy 4:12 instructs us to set an example in speech, in conduct, in faith, in love, and in purity. The Lord doesn't tell us to wait until our brother treats us nicely for us to act in a way that glorifies Him; rather, He commands us to set an example. Practically, setting the example meant me respecting my brother, speaking to him in the way I wanted to be spoken to, encouraging him, and choosing to spend time with him.

2. **Intentionally interact.** When I was boiling over with hatred for my brother, the last thing I wanted to do was spend time with him. But that was exactly what I needed to do. Relationships exist as a result of time being invested. Intentionally, I spent time doing things with my brother that he liked doing. I took time to get to know him — reading books, playing a game, going for a bike ride outside.

3. **Wielding my words.** Proverbs 18:12 says that our words have the power of life and death, and those who love it will eat its fruit. I love power. And I used the power of my words. Unfortunately, I took way too many opportunities to slice and stab my brother with

my words rather than protect and encourage him. As I chose to change, I frequently had to say nothing. But as I learned to encourage my brother with my words, I have seen him stand taller, treat others more gently, and respect me.

4. **Pray.** There is nothing you can do that will produce more result than prayer. Pray for your siblings. Pray for yourself. Pray. Pray. Pray. And pray some more. God knows your heart better than you, and He knows what your siblings need more than you ever will. Talking to your all-knowing Creator is never a waste of time. Tell Him, when you're struggling, just how much you hate your brother or sister (after all, it's better to tell Him than yell at your sibling), and ask Him to give you the grace and humility to rebuild or maintain your relationship with the person He has put in your life.

There are a lot of things I hope you get from this chapter, but if you only get one thing, I hope it's this: the most important relationships in your life, besides your relationship with Jesus Christ, are in your home. I never desired to be best friends with my siblings. That wasn't "cool." But today, I would choose spending time with my brothers and sisters over spending time with most anyone.

My siblings are my friends, my confidantes, and the people who know me better than I know myself. They know my weaknesses, strengths, ugliness, and vulnerability, yet they love me and support me.

Imperfect Diamond

Today, that brother who made my blood boil is one of my closest friends. Frequently, he comes to me for advice, encouragement, and prayer. Even more exciting is that Ben now comes to me for relationship advice because, ironically, one of his younger brothers makes his blood boil, too.

And you know what, I have answers for him, not because I was always the perfect sister, but because I was the imperfect sister who heard God tell her that there was more. I was the imperfect sister who dared to believe more was possible even if it took four apologies and years to experience restoration.

So, if you've been an imperfect sister like me, don't give up. God doesn't call the equipped. He equips the called. If you have siblings, you are called to be a sister. Therefore, your God will equip you.

Don't be afraid of being imperfect; rather, embrace the imperfection and let God perfect both you and your relationship. Just as a diamond begins as a crusty, cold clump of coal, but emerges from furious flames as a solid, sparkling stone, so our imperfection, when resigned to God's perfection, becomes a brilliant testimony and enduring relationship.

God's power is at work within you (Eph. 3:20). So, instead of letting your blood boil with hatred, allow the power of God to boil over inside of you, overwhelming your relationship with your siblings, and He will do exceedingly, abundantly more than you could ever ask or imagine (Eph. 3:20).

Another Talent

And finally, know this: your sibling relationships are one of the "talents" that God has given you to steward well for His glory. In our culture it's easy to push our siblings away, but when we do, we are pushing away one of our *such a time* moments.

Being a brother or sister isn't just a birth occurrence — it is a responsibility, privilege, and blessing. If you have siblings, you can be certain that your *such a time* is staring you in the face. So, abandon any *someday-when* thoughts that you might be holding onto and embrace your *such a time* to join the Lord in making your sibling everything God has planned for him or her to be.

It was when I embraced the *such a time* in my relationships with my siblings that I went from a hate-filled beginning to power-filled friendships. Good thing too because it wasn't long before my sisters started wearing my clothes and dressing like me. Shortly after that, my dance students were picking out "Sisi clothes" at Goodwill. With my sisters at my side, I was able to explore what beauty meant and how to dress as "His Girl" for *such a time*.

REFLECT

Read Proverbs 17:17.

Which of the 4 "getting practical" steps do you need to work on most?

Write down how you are going to do that for the rest of the week.

SUCH A WARDROBE

I've come to realize that what I wear is more than just a barrier between my body and the public, but can actually be a testimony to all I believe about beauty and its Creator.
~Trina Holden~

Once upon a time, there was a girl who loved clothes and beautiful things. As soon as she knew what makeup was, she begged to wear it. Finally, she got her first makeover and her very own makeup set when she turned thirteen. At fifteen, she dreamed of being a model, posing with a fan, tossing her billowing locks, and being on the cover of *Vogue*. Dress-up was still one of her favorite pastimes at twenty-one. Today, even though she's as much an adult as any and has deserted the idea of being on the cover of *Vogue*, she still loves clothes and beautiful things . . .

In case you're wondering—I'm the girl who begged to wear makeup and grew into the adult who still loves to play dress-up. Recently, I have been wondering, "What does God think is beautiful? Is it wrong to dress

beautifully?" So, I asked Him. And this is what He told
me . . .

> *I made you to be who you are in me: victorious, fearless,
> beautiful, stunning, bold, gentle, wise, calm, and powerful.
> All these things are facets of me.*
>
> *I made art and colors and patterns. I want you to love art —
> create, design, explore, and experiment with it. Use it to
> express who I am in you. It's part of what I made you to do.*
>
> *I attract you with my nature, rainbows, and sunsets. I tell
> you who I am through flowers and hurricanes. I reveal myself
> to you through the ocean's mighty waves.*
>
> *Yes, use beauty, use art, use fashion — love and enjoy them
> because they are tools that I have given you to express who I
> am in you.*

Hearing this was like a breath of fresh air. I was
inspired. Not only did God create beauty, but He
delights when I enjoy it and use it. When I dress
beautifully, I am putting a facet of Christ on display.
Trina Holden, prolific author and blogger, said it this
way:

> I've come to realize that what I wear is more than just a barrier between my body and the public, but can actually be a testimony to all I believe about beauty and its Creator.

Ultimately, clothing, modesty, and fashion really have nothing to do with us. Beauty and what we wear has everything to do with God. When we dress well, we are expressing a facet of His beauty to others.

Tools in Our Closets

Clothes are tools we have been given to present His beauty to others. As with all tools, there are multiple ways to use them correctly and incorrectly. When I think of someone who uses her clothing and appearance in a positive manner, Kate Middleton instantly comes to mind.

All eyes have been on Kate Middleton since she began dating Prince William in 2003 and even more so since her engagement and marriage. Neither her actions nor appearance has let us down.

While tabloids have been anxious to jump at any scooping neckline or knee sighting, she has graciously represented herself and the British government with style and dignity. Her wardrobe selection is a style of its own, including colors, lace, jewels, and varying hem lengths, all the while, never lacking decent propriety.

Clearly, Kate understands that her appearance no longer reflects her alone, as it did in college. Her wardrobe choice elevates the reputation of Prince William and the entire royal family. As a result, headlines praise her for her elegant, dignified, and grace-filled style.

But, can you imagine the headlines if she wore a dress, just once, like Kim Kardashian? What would the Queen Mother say?! I have no doubt that Kate's choice in such a circumstance would exemplify her quality sense of style, but she would sacrifice the dignity of the British royalty as well as her own. The Internet would explode, not to mention every magazine in every checkout line would be covered with the "scandal."

Dressing More Than Ourselves

Similarly, when we become a "His Girl," our clothes no longer represent ourselves alone. Our appearance impacts the reputation of God, in whose image we are created. It is critical that we understand, just as Kate Middleton does, the impact our wardrobe choices make on everyone around us – good and bad – so that we can use the impact to exalt our Creator, who is both beautiful and dignified.

So, how can we represent our God well in the same way that Kate Middleton represents her royal family with dignity? That's a great question and a fun one. I'm glad you asked.

Let's take our hints from the Duchess herself, shall we?

She Dresses Beautifully

The most beautiful things don't ask for attention.
~"The Secret Life of Walter Mitty"~

Kate's wardrobe choices aren't always the most fashionable or created by the most known designer. But you can always count on Kate's choice to be beautiful. Kate demonstrates that beauty is style that never goes out of fashion. Accordingly, she chooses clothes that are beautiful. Like a flower, she doesn't ask for attention.

Whenever I try to dress in the most fashionable clothes, I find that I don't feel beautiful. I definitely don't feel like me. Instead, my reflection reminds me of my trendiest friends.

Unlike me, Kate doesn't mimic anyone's style. She dresses herself like herself. She artfully balances cutting-edge trends with her own style. It would have been easy for Kate to make her wardrobe a fashion runway, but instead, she has made it a representation of herself: feminine, classy, themes of red, blue, and black, simplistic, and delicately embellished. Best of all, her end result is always *beautiful.*

Although the most stylish pants today are skinny jeans, and most of my friends and all three of my sisters wear them—not me. The last thing I feel in skinny jeans is beautiful. Bell-bottoms and boot-cut for me, thank you very much.

On the other hand, my sisters would not be caught dead wearing my wide-legged pants. They are short, so bell-bottoms end up making them look shorter. The last thing they feel in bell-bottoms is beautiful. So, they don't wear them.

After all, fashion was made by women who decided that they felt beautiful in something other than what everyone else was wearing, and before long, everyone else was wearing what made the first lady feel beautiful. So be a trendsetter by wearing what makes you feel beautiful, whether or not it's on the runway!

When I made a Pinterest board, I found that my theme was bold, brilliant, and colorful. If you were to define my style, it would be: fearless grace—bold, brilliant, beautiful. While I LOVE Kate's style, it's just not me.

Look in my wardrobe and you will find stunning showstoppers. I like to dazzle and stun. Patterned pants are my friend. Embellished necklines are my favorite.

Long, flowing skirts are my jam. Statement necklaces are my hero.

I have found that when I forget trends and just wear what I feel most beautiful in, I get the most compliments. That's not to say, "Dress to get all the compliments." But remember, there is something unapologetically transfixing about beauty that is not defined by style or limited by fashion.

She Dresses with Dignity

> *In a world where everyone is overexposed*
> *the coolest thing you can do is*
> *maintain your mystery.*
> ~Pinterest~

You won't ever see Kate in a leather and sheer creation like Miley Cyrus. She knows that while exposing certainly draws attention, it does not kindle respect.

Imagine this . . . there is a delightful 10-year-old girl, we'll call her Bella, dressed in a flouncy, lacy pink dress with puffed sleeves and a billowing pink satin bow in her blonde hair. Everyone who passes whispers, "Lovely! Precious! Totes adorbs!" Suddenly, she's rolling around in the mud, bashing her head on the ground, screaming and flailing! So much for all her bows and lace! Now everyone from a mile's radius is staring, including you, as you wonder how you could have ever thought her to be lovely.

When we wear plunging necklines, sheer bodices, or ultra-tight pants, we are acting like the dolled-up 10-year-old having a tantrum. Ignoring the softly whispered remarks on our beauty, we trade our dignity for attention. We flaunt ourselves and make an episode attracting everything but respect! I love the way Ezekiel puts it on the blog *The Full Time Girl* (www.thefulltimegirl.com):

> When a woman considers modesty in relation to her appearance, she doesn't just command attention and a few stares. She commands respect and admiration. The way a woman dresses shows her values and her standards, it shows how much she values herself . . . *modesty depicts worth.*

Kate's wardrobe consistently enunciates dignity. People notice. Her elegance is far from unnoticed. On the contrary, her ability to consistently dress fabulously while kindling respect draws plenty of attention and has dresses flying off the racks!

I must admit that merging dignity and beauty has been a journey for me. In high school, deep V necklines, tight tops, and form-fitting jeans were my favorite. I thought I looked beautiful in them, but the truth was I knew I got more attention when I wore them. I fell for the world's lie that lustful glances from others meant I looked beautiful. Sorry to burst your bubble, but those lustful looks translate to "People are 'seeing' things they shouldn't be."

> A woman doesn't need to expose her body
> to be beautiful.
> –Christopher (www.thefulltimegirl.com)

Sexy isn't the same as *beautiful*. Don't be the said dolled-up 10-year-old throwing a tantrum and confuse *sexy* with *lovely*. There is a time and place for "hot" but that's in your bedroom with your husband, not on the playground in the mud or in the grocery aisle at Walmart (wrong aisle, ladies).

When we choose to dress in a dignified manner, we silently communicate that there's more than meets the eye. And, that there's more to us than curves and makeup. I love this encouragement from Ken on *The Full Time Girl* blog:

> Simply put, I am way more attracted to the woman who carries herself with respect than the girl who seeks attention. The woman who catches my eye is the one so wrapped up in her goals, dreams, ambitions, and definitely in God that she doesn't care about the attention of others. How does this relate to modesty? The modest woman will dress for what she has to DO that day while the attention seeking girl dresses for

WHO sees HER that day. *I want a woman that is going places and so doesn't place value on who is watching her go there.* That's whom I am attracted to.

Such A Time

As stated on *InsideOut*'s "About" fashion page:

From the fig leaves in the Garden of Eden to the catwalks of New York City, fashion has always been the outward expression of the heart of a culture. We all know not to "judge a book by its cover," but what's often overlooked is the fact that the cover can give you a good idea of what's inside. In Christian-speak, it's not enough to claim that, "It's the heart that counts," and, therefore, clothes and style don't matter.

Because they do.

Each of these style icons—Audrey Hepburn, Jackie Onassis, and Cary Grant—realized that it is the person who matters, not the clothes. But also that clothes are an integral part of showing the world who you are. In the words of Miuccia Prada:

What you wear is how you present yourself to the world, especially today, when human contacts are so quick. Fashion is instant language.

> The statement our clothing makes should be in synchrony with what we believe. If Christ has renewed our hearts, then our fashion needs to reflect that. There doesn't have to be a trade off of either fashion or faith. Quite the opposite: Our style should help us shine for Christ. High fashion with high standards is a witness to our King. (https://insideoutstyleandfashion.word press.com/about/)

From this day forward, I am committed to high fashion with high standards because what I wear is not about me and my beauty; it's about High King Jesus and His beauty. What I wear is an instant message to everyone who sees me, communicating what I believe and to whom I belong.

Being featured on the cover of *Vogue* is no longer my aspiration. Instead, through my love of clothes and beautiful things, I strive to dress in such a way that those who see me think well of my Creator, just as Kate makes the world think well of the British government and her husband.

Instead of waiting for *someday when* fashion is beautiful and modest to represent Christ well through our wardrobe, I challenge you to seize the *such a time* you are given every morning. When you step into your closet to choose an outfit, ask yourself how you can represent your Almighty Creator to the best of your ability.

God created beauty and makes our heart gasp in awe when we see something truly beautiful. It is now our responsibility and privilege to present this same beauty through what we wear and how we present ourselves. Checking ourselves in the mirror is *such a time* for giving the best first impression of our Creator as possible.

But *such a time* doesn't end with our morning mirror check or latest shopping spree; *such a time* also includes the skills we gather and how we earn money.

REFLECT

What do you feel most beautiful in? What makes you feel like "you"? Make a list or pull out of all the clothes that make you say, "That's how I want people to think of me," "That's makes me feel like 'me,'" or "I feel beautiful!"

Maybe even start a Pinterest board. What is the common theme? Are they athletic clothes with a sporty headband? Is it jeans, T-shirt, and a cardigan? Maybe, a skirt and a blouse, with a casual jacket and heels? You might even find that all your favorite clothes are brilliant blue. Forget about fashion for a moment. Just be beautiful — beYOUtiful!

Ask yourself and honestly answer: "Do I dress beautifully and with dignity?"

If not, what do you need to do to dress like yourself while expecting respect?

If so, how can you encourage others to do similarly?

SUCH A BUSINESS

She considers a field and buys it;
out of her earnings she plants a vineyard.
She makes linen garments and sells them,
and supplies the merchants with sashes.
~Proverbs 31:16 & 24~

All growing up, I dreamed of being a waitress. Taking orders in a classy outfit with shiny black heels and serving dinner at a nice restaurant with cloth tablecloths was exactly what I had in mind. "What a fun way to earn money," I thought.

But my mother challenged my girly dreams. She challenged me to think outside of the box and beyond a minimum-wage job. She dared me to not only earn money but to develop skills. Pondering my mom's brilliant approach to earning money, I was inspired by my dear friend Lindsey who took earning money to a whole new level.

While still in high school, Lindsey saved money and invested in two dogs. Before long, she had taught herself how to breed dogs and vaccinate their puppies. Then she sold the puppies. Shortly after, she became a Mary Kay consultant, helping women select and apply makeup.

During this time, she not only learned valuable skills in marketing, dog education, responsibility, how to do her makeup really, REALLY well, and handling money, but she was able to save enough money to put a cash down payment on her and her husband's first home as well as purchase their first set of couches.

The time Lindsey invested in entrepreneurial endeavors during high school set her marriage and household up for financial success. She was ready for *such a time*. Today she manages a household of seven, homeschools her five children, and supports her husband in his personal business.

In the case of my friend Lindsey, she knew when she was sixteen that she was going to marry Daniel. It is a love-at-first-sight kinda story, if you know what I mean! She realized that her *such a time* was the fact that she knew whom she was going to marry at such a young age. Her *such a time* was preparing. Therefore, everything she pursued was with the hope of preparing for a successful future with the love of her life, financially and skillfully.

Skillfully

The skills and financial blessing Lindsey was able to bring into her family remind me of the Proverbs 31 woman. In Proverbs 31, King Lemuel describes a woman who not only brings her husband good *all* the days of her life (before and after marriage) but is also industrious. She is the one who works with eager hands, prepares good food, invests wisely, works vigorously, is prepared for her tasks, has profitable trading, watches over the affairs of her household, and is not idle (Proverbs 31:13–18, 24, 27). She is praised for her ability to raise a family and run a business.

The skills Lindsey developed allowed her to not only build a successful financial future for her family but also serve her as she manages her household and helps her husband run their business. Because she spent time developing business skills in high school, she does not have to acquire those skills now. Instead, she is able to work alongside her husband in his business and still raise her family. She might not ever breed dogs again or open a makeup studio, but the skills she learned have made her an industrious woman.

As young women, we do not yet have the responsibility of running a household, supporting a husband, and raising a family. We have time and energy to invest. How much better to learn how to run a business without these responsibilities so that you can use the skills when you do have a laundry list of responsibilities? Taking advantage of not having the responsibility of running a household and investing our time into growing skills will help us have strong arms for our tasks in the future (Proverbs 31).

More Than Money

At some point during high school, usually around the time we get our driver's license, we are encouraged to get a job. Off to Chick-fil-A or Aéropostale we go! But I would like to challenge you to think beyond a normal minimum-wage job. There's nothing wrong with getting a job at Chick-fil-A. I'm sure you'll learn more than how to make lemonade.

But what if you could get a job that would contribute to more than just your bank account or gas fund? I want you to think bigger. Think long term. Think about impacting a community or changing lives. Think of gaining an arsenal of skills.

The following stories are of young women who overstepped the status quo and lived for *such a time*. They are women who weren't okay with a retail or fast food occupations. These are women who didn't just earn some extra cash. They decided to grow a skill set through their job that could benefit them in the future. In the process, each of them has made a difference in her life, the lives around her, and her future life.

One of my sister's best friends, **Kimmy**, got a job with a catering company. Through her job, she learned new recipes, how to keep food warm, transport food, serve food, present food, make large amounts, and how to please customers. By the time you purchase and read this book, she will be a newly married bride, running a household of her own. Cooking will be an invaluable tool in her new season of life.

Samantha, a friend of mine, loved baking treats with flour she milled at home. So, with her brothers and sisters, they started a bakery of sorts where families could make weekly orders of fresh, homemade baked goods. Before too long, they began attending farmers markets. It's more than earning money for Samantha; it's learning how to manage a team, work with her family, and run a business.

Jasmine's father, Voddie Bauchman, is a prominent preacher in Texas as well as an author. Before long, Jasmine's passion for research propelled her father's writing career as she researched topics for his books. Working together, they were even able to create an online store. Sometimes it's as simple as using your passion to help someone close to you.

Hannah, another friend of mine, recently established her own clothing line: *Hannah Everly.* Just a few years ago she discovered her love for creating a wearable creation out of a bolt of material. With her sewing machine and

Etsy, she has created a successful skirt line that has been featured on "Classy Girls Wear Pearls" (www.classy-girlswearpearls.com), and has been worn by many bridesmaids, sororities, and friends from here and there and everywhere! *Hannah Everly* is now a popular trend!

My inspiring author friend, **Rachel**, also Hannah's sister, loved photography. Throughout high school, I never saw her without her camera. The first shoot she shadowed was my senior portrait session, which led to her eventually co-shooting a wedding with the same photographer. Before long, Rachel was shooting her own senior portraits, Christmas photos, and weddings. Now she coaches young photographers in what she loves most. Not only does she do something she loves and earns money, but she helps others do the same.

My sisters and I made meals as fundraisers to finance our attendance at camps with TeenPact, a leadership school my family is involved with. Buying food and cooking food were second nature to us. However, marketing, delivering, and accounting were another story! But week after week, as we collected orders and prepared sometimes up to 100 meals, we learned life-long skills and were able to pay for attending four camps!

Zipporah, once my harp student and now my prayer partner, has been working for my mom for the last year. Every morning she arrives at 9:30 am. Teaching math, tutoring writing, cooking lunch, and correcting spelling consume her time until she leaves at 12:30 pm. Daily, she is learning firsthand what running a household and homeschooling require. The coordination, multitasking, and attention to detail she is learning will also only benefit her with her own household someday.

When I was fifteen, I became a dance instructor at a local worship dance ministry. Two years later, I became the artistic director. Teaching dance was the smallest part of my job. I learned how to choreograph, plan performances, coordinate dress rehearsals, book facilities, work with parents, as well as train and lead instructors to the same vision. Through teaching dance, I not only learned valuable skills applicable for the rest of my life, but I have had the privilege of teaching many students how to worship the Lord through worship dance and established a legacy that will outlive me.

Five years ago, with my dad and sisters, I started Footprints Dance Ministry where we teach social etiquette and dance skills through ballroom dance twice a month. Before long, I was the executive director coordinating not only the bi-monthly events, including two balls a year, but also a team of youth to pull off the night. Investing time into this ministry has stretched me more than I can ever describe. I have not only taught dance (again), but ordered snacks, enforced dress codes, coordinated chaperones, become a board member as well as learned to delegate and lead a team of leaders. It may be a volunteer position, but these skills will surely come in handy someday if I become the First Lady . . . !

Doing What You Love

One and a half years ago I decided to become a personal trainer. My mom had a friend who owned a personal training studio and is very successful in our community. So, I went to her studio and introduced myself. I asked for her guidance in becoming a personal trainer and what I needed to do to work for her someday. Within a month, she had recommended several certifications to me and I was shadowing (the equivalent to interning in the fitness world) at her studio. She asked that I have six months of experience after getting certified before I work with her and recommended several gyms for me to get experience.

Find someone you know or that a friend knows who has experience in your interests. Pick their brain. Ask for guidance and recommendations. Listen to them tell stories about their job. If they own a small business, have connections ask if you can work for or intern with them.

Think outside of the box. Internships aren't for everyone and every interest. Getting a job may be the best answer for you. Sometimes it's as simple as starting a blog and posting your fashion updates or newest recipes. Sell Pampered Chef! You want to be an event planner? Plan parties of your own and help with church events! It doesn't have to be "official" or include wearing shiny black heels.

Oftentimes, these skills will come in handy before you are married or helping your husband with a business. Recently, I was asked to be the state coordinator for a leadership school called TeenPact. Having been involved with TeenPact as a student and then as a staffer throughout high school, I was thrilled by the challenge. After just completing my second year as state coordinator, I cannot count the skills I use running the event, skills I've been gathering through selling meals as fundraisers, working as a personal trainer, and running a ballroom dance ministry.

Even if I never get married or my husband never has a personal business that I can help him with, I will not regret the time and energy I invested into my education through the jobs that I chose because the skills that I have gained far outweigh the money I may have earned waitressing. And, who knows, I may have earned more!

Another Talent

Do you remember the story I shared in chapter one about the men who invested their talents and the one who buried his? This is one of the most tangible ways we get to invest the "talent" our Master, Jesus Christ, has given us. The men in the story didn't know what they would receive as a result of investing well. They were simply faithful. Later, they were rewarded accordingly. This reminds me of Lydia. Her story is recorded in Acts 16:

> 13 On the Sabbath we [Paul and Silas] went outside the city gate to the river, where we expected to find a place of prayer. We sat down and began to speak to the women who had gathered there. 14 One of those listening was a woman from the city of Thyatira named Lydia, a dealer in purple cloth. She was a worshiper of God. The Lord opened her heart to respond to Paul's message. 15 When she and the members of her household were baptized, she invited us to her home. "If you consider me a believer in the Lord," she said, "come and stay at my house." And she persuaded us.
>
> Later during their stay in Macedonia Paul and Silas were captured, imprisoned, and put on trial. Finally, when their Roman citizenship was discovered they were released.
>
> 40 After Paul and Silas came out of the prison, they went to Lydia's house, where they met with the brothers and sisters and encouraged them.

The most frustrating part about living for *such a time* is the temptation to live for *someday when*. That's not what Lydia did. Lydia *lived* her *such a time*. I hardly think she knew that on that particular Sabbath she would meet

Paul and Silas, who would soon desperately need her support. Surely, she could not have seen her home becoming a meeting place for believers and being recorded in the Bible for us to read thousands of years later.

It was her intentional living—the way that she lived, aware that every moment, every day, every Sabbath meeting, every customer she dealt with, and every dinner party she threw was her *such a time*. She didn't live every activity and chore as if it were for *someday when*. Instead she lived it as *today*. As a result, she was prepared. Her business supplied her with a home, people skills, and the capability to host others.

It's the same with us. We don't know the ins and outs of our life. And thank goodness because if we did have a map of our life, we wouldn't need God. We would be God. While we don't have a map, we have each been given a talent, just like Lydia. It is to live for *such a time* today—investing the talent well—that will allow us to be prepared.

Lindsey, myself, and each of the girls I mentioned didn't have all the dots connected. We still don't. But we know and trust with all our hearts that God will make the completed picture exceedingly, abundantly, and above all that we can imagine (Eph 3:20).

Exactly, how He will do that, we're willing to leave up to Him because we don't have the map, and, quite honestly, we think we would do a pretty bad job at being "God." But we are determined to do our part. We are daring to connect the two dots we can see to the best of our ability, knowing that this is our *such a time*.

So, even if your husband never has a business that you help him with, you still haven't wasted your time. You've earned money for furthering your education, growing your skills, and intentionally investing that talent that was given to you.

It's more than earning money. It's more than doing something you love. It's more than gaining skills. It's about being the best steward of your time as possible. It's about living in *such a time* for *such a time*.

As I look back on all the opportunities I invested in, one of the most important parts of my growth has been my mentors. After all, without my mom I would have had a little waitressing job! Seeking out and respecting mentors is critical to your ability to live for *such a time*.

P.S. Before I conclude this chapter I would like to remind you of a key phrase in the Proverbs 31 woman's long list of productivity: "She watches over the affairs of her household." Even in the midst of her making crowd-pleasing meals, being prepared for her tasks, and earning money, none of this happens at the expense of her family. As long as these ventures enhance her family, she's a powerhouse, but if at any point these ventures compromise the integrity of her family, her attentions will be redirected. As a wife and mom, her number one priority, her God-given talent for this season of her life, is her family. That's what Paul was pointing out in 1 Corinthians 7, "But a married woman is concerned about the affairs of this world—how she can please her husband." The talent entrusted to a wife and a mom is that of wife and mom. She must intentionally invest in them before she invests in anything else.

REFLECT

Read Proverbs 31:10–31.

What do you LOVE to do? Is it sewing, writing, crafting, hosting tea parties, exploring the wilderness, working out, cooking, researching? Make a list of five things you love to do.

How can you apply what you love or are interested in to the next level either by investing in others or growing the skills to invest in the future?

MENTORS

Teach the older women to be reverent in the
way they live . . . , but to teach what is good.
Then they can urge the younger women
to love their husbands and children.
~Titus 2:3~

Living for *such a time* is hard. It's not easy to wait well or connect the dots in our lives. It's easy to lose our way, get distracted, or just plain get confused. I call it— Distorted Perspective, Lack of Perspective, and Fractured Perspective. In these moments, my mentors, primarily Trish and Mom, have been my comfort and compass, encouraging me and pointing me "due north" as I seek to live for *such a time*.

The following is a snapshot from a recent correspondence via texting with my mentor, Trish, while I was working as state coordinator:

Me: Can you talk in an hour?

Trish: No, I'm driving to a tournament. Can you talk now? I'll be driving for another hour.

Me: No, we have a speaker, and I need to thank her and escort her out. I'll be okay . . .

Trish: I'm praying for you.

Me: Thanks.

[*Twenty minutes later . . .*]

Me: Can you talk now? I just walked the speaker out.

Trish: Sure!

[**Ring, ring . . .*]

Trish: Hey, how are you?

Me: Well . . . ha . . . um . . . I'm not okay.

Trish: So, what's going on?

Me: First, there was a miscommunication, and there were not enough seats for me to get to the capitol. So, I missed the first speaker. Then, I miscounted the lunches, and we were one short. Then I went on a field experience and totally forgot that there was another speaker. I got back to find everyone was waiting on me. I introduced myself to the speaker, and she said that she had emailed me her PowerPoint

presentation—the reason why everyone was waiting for me.

Trish: Samantha, I think a lot of these problems would not have happened if you weren't struggling physically right now.

Me: You're right, but the state coordinator is supposed to be the one SOLVING all the problems, not CAUSING all the problems!

Trish: Samantha, I think you need to walk in humility here. Is anyone else upset with you?

Me: No. I don't think most of them even realize . . . maybe two of them.

Trish: Then, I understand how you are feeling, but you need to relax and let God be in control. Remember, in your weakness He is strong.

Me: Yeah . . .

[*10 minutes and many tears later . . .]

Trish: Are you okay?

Me: [Huge inhale . . .] Yes.

Trish: Can I pray?

Me: That would be great!

Mentors provide perspective and stability. When I'm in the middle of my life, I lose my perspective. There are so many decisions to make in this season that I often feel out of control. And, so often I get confused. Throughout the years, my parents and Trish have been my compass to life. As the ocean of life tosses me to and fro, they always point me true north.

Just like Mordecai admonished Esther, "And who knows but that you have come to your royal position for such a time as this?" my mentors have faithfully directed me to my *such a time*. They rarely give me the answer, but they faithfully remind me of the truth. Their wisdom has been invaluable to me.

Like a compass, mentors are trustworthy and reliable. They have been tested and tried. It doesn't mean that they're flawless human beings, but their goal and motives are right.

Two things I know for sure about my parents and mentor are: 1) They love Jesus and want His will and glory more than anything else, and 2) they love me and only want what's best for me. Being confident of these two things allows me to be able to receive what they tell me even when it's uncomfortable and I don't like it.

Consulting the Compass

While searching for water, which is due north, in a scorching desert, you're not going to be thrilled when you look at your compass and realize that you have been walking to the east of the precious H2O for the previous two hours! Even though you may be devastated and offended, you will not question your compass. Instead, you will reroute your course.

In the same way, when you know beyond a shadow of a doubt that your mentors love God and love you, you will be able to receive their direction even if it means rerouting your life.

One of the most difficult things for me to remember is that mentors are not my GPS; they are my compass. A mentor's' job is not to solve your problems or to give you the answer. John 14:14 says, "Know the truth and the truth will set you free." The job of a mentor is to influence your decision by guiding and supporting you, providing information, and, most importantly, by reminding you of the truth.

Mirages of Life

Most of the decisions I have made post-high school have been between good thing #1 and good thing #2. Will I work as a personal trainer or accept an internship? Will I stay home for the summer and run dance camps and hang out with my siblings, or be a camp counselor?

These are the mirages of life. There's not really a right or wrong answer. There simply is a *better* answer. Unfortunately for me, more often than not, the better answer has been the answer that is outside my comfort zone. That's where mentors come in. They can often see the better answer and are not inhibited by my comfort zone because, more than anything else, they want the best for me.

Trailblazing this new season of life with my mom and Trish, I have come to realize that, more often than not, like a mirage, it is my perspective that frustrates or confuses me. Mirages in life confuse us just as they do in the desert. My mentors have been invaluable because they have a clear perspective, an outside perspective, and a more complete perspective that allows them to see through the mirages that are disorienting me.

The three mirages I encounter are: Distorted Perspective, Lack of Perspective, and Fractured Perspective.

Distorted Perspective

As in the story that I opened the chapter with, sometimes a mirage is simply a loss of perspective. During the conversation I opened the chapter with, I was drowning in my mistakes, the fact that I had completely failed my job (or so it appeared to me in the moment), and how I had messed everything up for everyone!

What Trish saw was my physical weakness and God's power made perfect in my weakness. So, Trish directed me to 2 Corinthians where Paul explains that he rejoices in suffering, temptation, and persecution because it is in his weakness that God's strength is made perfect.

I have always been a little frustrated by this verse. Why on earth would I WANT to be tempted? I certainly don't want to throw a party every time I'm hurting. But reading it this time, I realized that Paul wasn't rejoicing because of pain or temptation. Rather, he was rejoicing because his weakness and mistakes allowed God's glory to shine even more.

I was focused on myself, how I had messed up, how I had let people down. Paul was focused on how God made everything come together for good, how God opened prison doors, and how God proved His power.

Trish didn't tell me my focus was wrong. She merely pointed me in the right direction. Because her viewpoint regarding my life is different from mine, she was able to see that I wasn't the problem. My distorted perspective was the problem. My mistakes were so blown up from my viewpoint that I couldn't see God glorifying Himself in me, which was all I really wanted.

The correct perspective, which Trish saw, was that I was making mistakes, but God was bigger than the mistakes. In fact, He was so much bigger than the mistakes that they were actually an opportunity for God to show Himself powerful and grow and unite the team. Looking back, I realize that hardly anyone else even noticed the mistakes that were distorting my perspective.

When our perspective is distorted, all we can see is the problem. That's when we need a mentor to reel us in and refocus our perspective by pointing us in the right direction.

Lack of Perspective

Recently, I got a job as a personal trainer at a local gym, which also happened to be the gym I always wanted to work at! Before signing the paperwork, I spent a month seeking the Lord about whether or not I should take the job.

In my original pursuit of the job, I was expecting to work about five hours a week, not ten. My parents strongly encouraged me to take the job, and I believed that the Lord had confirmed that I should explore this new territory called *JOB*. So, I signed the paperwork and began wearing my red shirt and black exercise pants.

About three months into the job, I was discouraged and frustrated. I had lost two clients, and the other members

SUCH A TIME

I met with were not interested or financially able to pay for training. I began to feel as though I was a bad trainer and that I was not achieving my goals. That's when Mommy and Trish asked me, "What were your goals when you took the job?"

To be honest, my goal when I took the job was not to become the head trainer and impress everyone there with the amount of clients and steady schedule I maintained. All I wanted was to learn how to create a workout plan, how to interact with clients, and how to be a good trainer.

The next question they asked was, "Are you meeting your goals?"

To which I had to answer, "Yes!" Yes, I was achieving everything I had set out to gain and accomplish. Would I have liked to have more clients and earn more money? Of course, but that wasn't the goal. I had lost my perspective.

Losing my perspective discouraged and distracted me from my purpose. My discouragements led me to beg my mom to support me in quitting my job. Thankfully, she said no, reminding me that I had prayed about this job and my goals were being achieved.

When I signed the paperwork and tried on my uniform, I knew what my goal was. As the days turned to weeks and the weeks turned to months, I lost my perspective. I forgot that the reason I took this job was to gain experience.

My frustration and discouragement mounted as I let my goals be replaced by pressure to have ten training appointments a week. Mom didn't necessarily know why I wanted to quit, but she knew my original goal and that I was achieving it. She saw my goals being met while I saw nothing happening because I had lost my perspective. Because my Mom was able to see the whole picture, she was able to fill in the lines where my perspective was lacking.

Fractured Perspective

Can you imagine doing everything that you love and always dreamed of all day every day? For the last two years I haven't had to imagine at all. I teach worship dance, mentor high school girls, read to my siblings, cook breakfast for my mom, work for my dad, run a ballroom dance ministry for youth, train for triathlons, play the harp professionally, and participate in ToastMasters. My life is the epitome of my dream come true! But last semester I felt as though I was living a nightmare. I felt like I was groping through thick fog desperately trying navigate my *such a time*. I felt defeated and unfulfilled.

SUCH A TIME

I couldn't understand why suddenly I didn't want to teach dance, I hated cooking, and reading to my siblings had become stressful. My perspective was fractured because I was not clinging to the truth that God is more than enough and that He is always working everything out for the good of those who love Him.

As I wrestled with my dream-come-true-life-turned-nightmare, my mom faithfully listened to me rant, bawl, and sigh. Day after day, week after week, she patiently reminded me of the truth: the truth that I was living my dream life, I had prayed and sought the Lord about every activity in my life before I added it to my schedule, and that there is *always* enough time to do the will of God (Elisabeth Elliot).

Gradually, as the truth seeped into the cracks of my perspective, I realized that I had let lies creep into my heart and mind that fracture my perspective. These lies are what led me to believe that my life was too much and that God was too little.

My mom saw that my life wasn't the problem. My activities were not making me feel miserable. And, my full schedule was not stealing my passion. She saw that it was my *perspective* that was destroying my perfect life. Because of her outside perspective, she was able to see what I couldn't and remind me of the truth.

One of my favorite verses says, "Know the truth and the truth will set you free." When my mom reminded of the truth, which then filled in the cracks of my fractured perspective, I was free to fully live my dream-come-true life.

Finding A Mentor

Stepping off the plane after a summer at JH Ranch in California, one of my goals was to find a mentor. I assumed it would include talking to several of the women I admired and asking them to be my mentor. That's not how it went at all.

I was talking with my friend Trish one day and simply asked if she would be willing to call me each week to just talk and pray. She readily agreed, and we picked a time: Wednesday, 8:30 am. In fact, we just had a phone call and prayer this morning!

Every week we call. She listens to the new developments, victories, and struggles of my life. Then we exchange prayer requests. It's a pretty simple deal. But it's consistent and centered around Christ. Sometimes we talk for fifteen minutes, other days for an hour, depending on our availability and my need for support.

SUCH A TIME

The most important thing to look for in a mentor is:
1) A sold-out love for Jesus Christ
2) Desire for God's will above anything else
3) Willingness to mentor and hold you accountable
4) Honesty and ability to speak even the hard truth
5) Commitment to pray

While there's a lot that comes from your mentor listening to you and offering wisdom, the benefits you'll receive from your mentor's sharing her own struggles are equally valuable. Learning from the life experience of another woman, hearing how she responds to difficulties, and witnessing how she overcomes struggles will powerfully influence who you become. Life is not lived in words or idleness. Life is an active responsibility that happens in real time.

So, make sure your mentor is someone you admire and want to be like. Please don't go seeking a flawless mentor to imitate because, if you find one, you will have found a phony.

Instead, find a woman who seeks the Lord in her brokenness and trusts God to work all things together according to His good and perfect plan. Find someone who, although several years beyond you, is on a similar journey toward Christ, seeking His grace, glory, and sanctification.

SUCH A TIME

A broken woman, who lets Jesus put her together in the midst of her life, is who you want to be like anyway. Let's face it, we're never going to be the picture-perfect Proverbs 31 woman.

The woman whose story went down in history was a broken woman who poured out all she had at the feet of Jesus that He might be glorified. While everyone brushed her aside because of her brokenness, Jesus embraced her. That's what Jesus specializes in: taking brokenness and making it sparkle for Him like never before. So find a woman to mentor you who is determined to glorify God, no matter the cost.

Like me, you might find that it's simply a weekly phone call. Perhaps, it is a biweekly meeting at Panera over a steaming cup of chai. Whatever the meeting looks like, be sure that your destination is the glory of Jesus Christ. Wherever your meeting place is, be sure to bring your life—victories, failures, and concerns—to the foot of Christ.

Don't be afraid to share your distorted, lacking, and fractured perspectives with your mentor. That's why you have her—to remind you of the truth that sets you free.

It's easy to become distracted by *someday when*, so whether texting, chatting on the phone, or face to face at Panera, choose to receive the truth and wisdom of your mentors as if you were consulting a compass in the middle of the Sahara Desert—let them point you toward your *such a time*!

REFLECT

Read Titus 2:3.

Make a list of an ideal mentoring experience: who, how, when, where, and frequency.

Make a list of three people who could be your mentor.

1._____

2._____

3._____

Pick up your phone and call them. Ask them to be your mentor and describe what you would like the mentoring relationship to look like.

SUCH A WOMAN

Follow my example, as I follow the example of Christ.
~1 Corinthians 1:11~

So far I've told you a lot of my story, but I wanted to take this opportunity for you to read the stories of other young women. Women who have inspired me by their quest to live for *such a time*. More than anything, I want you to know that your *such a time* won't look like my *such a time*, and it's not supposed to. Living as His Girl requires original pursuit and purposeful fulfillment of God's expectations for your life.

It is my prayer that through these four stories you are refreshed and encouraged to pursue *such a time* boldly in your life.

Amanda Jade Cox

I met Jesus beneath the stars and humidity of a North Carolina summer. I had heard about Him. *He was good, He loved me, He was the forgiving kind,* they told me. But I spent many years chasing after vapors of dreams I thought would fulfill, satisfy, and inspire. It was the July of my fourteenth birthday, that I was finally ready. I didn't know for what; I just knew for *Whom*. Little did I know that the *Whom* I was giving my life to would lead me on a journey unlike any I had ever dreamed. A journey that required patience and trust that my passionate self had never become acquainted with.

Throughout highschool I had dreamed of spending my life out in the field on the missions. People were my passion. I saw myself attending a fancy Bible school about two hours away. With grand plans and high hopes, I applied and was accepted. But instead of exultation, I felt chaotic and discontent. Not only that, my parents asked me to take a year off of school and stay at home.

Instead of charging off with my grand plans, I chose to obey my parents. I believed that my parents are the people God put in my life to guide me in His ways. So, I stayed home.

Desperate to make something out of my life and determined not to be one of "those" homeschool graduates who twiddles her thumbs until Prince Charming rides in on a gallant steed, I got a job. I worked and saved money. Before that year was up, all that money I had saved allowed me to go the Ukraine and Nicaragua spreading the Gospel of Jesus Christ.

It was on these trips that the Lord opened my eyes to the depth of His love and compassion. It's one thing to read an article or hear a missionary describe the desolate souls and land of other countries, but it's an entirely different thing to experience it. Face-to-face with heart-wrenching need, I realized that the Lord had not called me to simply spread His word with people overseas. He called me to tangibly share His love and compassion with the nations.

While serving in the Ukraine, I also learned about Ignite, a missions school in California. Again, a spark glowed in my heart. When I expressed interest in attending Ignite to my parents, they were in favor of it. Admittedly, I found it odd that my parents were against my attending a missions school two hours from my home but supportive of my going to school 3,000 miles across the country. But now I know — that's how God works. He gives us peace when the time and place are right. It doesn't always make sense, but there's peace — an assurance of God's presence and direction.

I flourished in California. I had never known the depth and goodness of God. I treasured every moment I spent pouring over theology books and preparing interactive Bible lessons. And these weren't any felt-board lessons. No, they included songs and activities. I even learned how to write and rap songs! But it was also that year at home, when my heart cried, "No, Lord let me go!" that allowed me to grow so much.

It was that year at home in rickety Richmond, that year I never wanted, that gave me everything I ever wanted. Because it was in that place of desperation, when no dots connected and my dreams seemed to be settling around me like ashes, that my heart had to find something more. And the something more it found was Jesus.

God shipwrecked the contented seasons of my soul along islands of loneliness and despair. But it was then that He taught me what patience and trust in Him were. He became my anchor because there wasn't anything else. He laid a foundation of peace in my soul that has seen me through many trials and triumphs.

Remember how I wanted to minister to the nations? Well, today I'm married to the man of my dreams—a man after God's own heart. And, I still live in Richmond. Recently, God showed my husband and me that the nations are in our neighborhood. So, even though I never really left Richmond, I'm living God's call on my life by choosing to show the great love and compassion of God's heart to my neighbors—the nations in my backyard.

And, as I look up at the stars between the high rises of our apartment complex, I realize that my entire life and pursuit of Jesus cannot be limited to one or even a few descriptive words. Someone once told me that God was good, that He loved me, and that He was the forgiving kind. Now, I tell this to my neighbors because I know that *He is good*, *He loves me*, and *He is the forgiving kind.*

Now, imagine we're sitting at an eclectic coffee shop sipping our dark brew. This is what I want you to take away from my story: If there's one thing I learned on this voyage of shipwrecked dreams, it's that a good story is never rushed and God has a killer reputation for growing good things in time. And, His way is always best. So, if you feel lost in a fog of confusion and hopelessness, despairing of life ever looking like a cohesive story, you're not alone. Remember, feelings aren't reality. Hazy chaos will pass. Seek God with your whole heart, and He will not disappoint. Whatever season you are in, it is only a footnote in the grander story of your life that God is writing—and it's better than anything you can ever imagine, I promise!

Elani Garfield

In the fashion world, people suggest that having the perfect little black dress can change your life. I was never a believer in that until I wore the same little black dress for 100 days. Yes—in a row. That's getting ahead of my story though. And really, this isn't my story because there is an Author who is scripting a greater story and I'm just a character in it.

SUCH A TIME

When I was a little girl, I fell in love. I fell in love with a country and that place was India. Maybe it was the beautiful people and the culture that were so different from mine that drew me in, but, more than that, it was the fact that I asked God to put a specific country on my heart to pray for and invest in. When I felt Him whisper, *India,* I was sure I'd heard wrong since that country wasn't even on my radar. My parents had always wanted to go to China, so that's where I had thought I would go too. Come to find out—God had scripted India into my scene. I was just ten at the time, but from that point on, something in my heart turned on. While reading about Amy Carmichael, I dreamed about being her and helping countless orphans. I couldn't wait till I was old enough to go off to this place of colors and spices.

Sometimes though God derails your life. It's as intense as it sounds. So far, this has happened twice in my life, but I hardly think it's the last time. At the time, these moments or years can seem confusing and pointless, but they are never wasted. When I was sixteen, my life got put on another track that I wouldn't have chosen for myself. Slowly but simultaneously all at once, my health turned on me, and I became very ill.

For about four years, I lay in bed or stayed at home just getting by. All my dreams and plans had been stripped from me, along with so many basic things. The way I looked changed, my friends changed, my sleep changed, my food changed, and really everything changed. Nearly everything I had put my worth in was suddenly gone, even good things. Any passion, vision, or purpose for my life was suddenly a hazy fog of things in the past.

It was probably right about then that I started to question whether God had forgotten me. Have you ever felt that way? Well, if so, you're not alone. Of course, it's a lie to believe that thought since we would literally cease to be if God forgot about us, but it's still a thought that can creep in. There will be times in all of our lives where we have to let go of our ideals and dreams, and choose to let the Scriptmaker direct us. He can see the whole play at once. He's read it and knows how it ends because He wrote it. We can only see this act right now, maybe even just a few lines. Often we need to go through a questioning time to be able to see what's really important. More than that, we need to feel helpless.

Wait—what—*helpless*? Yes, we can have big, crazy, amazing dreams of things we want to do for God and his glory, but unless we are truly willing to do it in His strength, we're missing the point. God doesn't need us to do things for Him. He just wants us to love Him and enjoy Him and make Him known through that joy and passion. Even if you can't ever do one thing for God, you are still valuable. I believe that if we can grasp that, then we will be a force to be reckoned with.

SUCH A TIME

After being in bed for years, lying low, and learning to be with Jesus on a new level, I slowly started getting better. We still don't really know what went wrong. But remember, being derailed can be a bit messy, and I wasn't sure how to start picking up the pieces of life and actually living again in anything other than crisis mode. While I didn't want to keep going through that pain, I was finally thankful for it. Could I dream again? Could my pain have a purpose? Yes!

One thing that gave me hope along the way towards the end of my sickness was meeting a young woman who was battling cancer. She was just 17–18 at the time. My dad came home one day that I was feeling particularly sorry for myself and told me how this young girl was fighting for her life, and right then and there, that gave me some much-needed perspective. I couldn't get her out of my mind. For days I kept thinking about her and wanting to help. Then I remembered that I'd seen some hospital gowns that were incredibly cute and decided I needed to get her some. The only problem was that I had no money, and they were expensive. Sitting at the kitchen counter, I told my dad the dilemma, and he told me I should think outside the box. We came up with the idea to ask my friends to donate money toward it, and I was blown away by the response. Within a few hours, my amazing friends had given so much that we had a couple hundred dollars to buy not just one but two gowns!

Something ignited in my heart. I felt so amazed at how much joy it had all brought me. When I got to deliver the gowns and finally meet the lovely young woman, I knew that helping people was my passion. The thing that makes you light up or that you just can't stop thinking about or know you will regret if you don't do is a good sign of what your passions may be.

So where does that little black dress fit in? I mean hospital gowns are neat, but what about that dress project? Remember how I said my life has been derailed twice? Well, the dress project was the second time.

One sleepless night in January of 2011, I tossed and turned and finally switched on the lamp beside my bed in frustration. My heart was feeling restless, and I knew that a lot of fears held me back. I was afraid of failure, I was afraid of never doing anything outside my comfort zone, but I was more afraid of wasting my life. It was time for a change, and it needed to be drastic. I was just 22, but it was a moment I will never forget when God spoke to me about how I needed to act.

When I woke up the next morning to tell my parents what I was feeling, I was both excited and quiet-nervous. I needed to tell them what I'd written in my journal the night before. I knew they were probably going to think I was crazy. I thought I was crazy! So in our kitchen on a cold, dark morning, I told my parents that I wanted to raise $50,000 for orphans in India over a short amount of time by wearing the same dress for 100 days. I told them I was going to blog the journey and daily share how I styled the dress differently. They just looked at me and urged, "Go for it!"

Sometimes we don't get to make the choice that puts our life on a different path, but sometimes we get to partner with God to do things that will change our lives and the lives of others around us for eternity. 2011 was the year I made that choice to face some fears I had. I didn't have a blog, I didn't have a black dress, and I didn't have an organization to partner with, but I knew I just had to take the first step. My blog was my first step, and considering that I was terrified to comment on other people's blogs, let alone push the "publish" button on my own, this was a big step. Things fell into place, and, before I knew it, I was in the middle of my fundraiser. Guess what? I got to raise money for orphans in India! It didn't look like I would be able to do that in the beginning, but God worked it out and it was amazing!

The project wasn't easy. It was exciting but had its challenges. I think sometimes I assume that because God shows us what He wants us to do, that it's going to be a walk in the park or that we'll accomplish our goals easily, but that's not necessarily the case. I didn't raise the $50K in 100 days. People were generous, and, of course, God was gracious. We raised $31K, but I didn't reach the goal I had set. Here's what I did learn though—God wants us to trust Him and follow His lead, even (and especially) when things aren't going our way or don't make sense.

Now four years later, I'm still fundraising. The dress project ended, but my love for people in India grew. And you know what? We didn't get to the $50K mark, but we did get past the $90K mark. God used the fact that I couldn't go to India due to my health to do something even bigger than I had originally imagined. While I saw my health as an obstacle, God used it for good. If I would have gone to India, I wouldn't have done a fundraiser most likely.

What's right in front of you? God wants you to use that. Being faithful isn't necessarily easy, but it is being a good steward with what you have and that is beautiful.

Whatever it is, whether big or small, whether wearing the same dress or starting a business, whether going to college or serving your family, God has a plan for each of us, and when we walk faithfully, we're right where we need to be. God does want to use you. He wants to take this time, this season in your life, and do something beautiful and He will. It might not look like what you expect, but that doesn't mean it won't be good. Mostly He wants to have a personal relationship with you, and I can promise you this—it is the most rewarding thing you can do. If everything flows out of that, then you'll live a life of vision and passion for the right things—to love God and love people.

Elise Waldbeser

I do not know where to begin. These words convict, causing me to think and reflect on my life. How am I seeking to use my life and education for the Lord's glory? Shouldn't this be my life theme? Shouldn't I have so much to tell and write? But, the stories I am remembering now are more like moments which have been for God's glory, rather than a lifetime for Him. But, then I remember the gifts I have been given, the talents God has drawn out of me. Most prominent in my life— listening to people and making them feel loved. I have been humbled by the way God has used that in my life. Through Teenpact, the young and old at church, at work, at school. Where did it start?

My junior year of high school was my very favorite! It was the year I was sixteen. My school schedule was established, and while I was taking hard classes, God was changing my perspective towards them. The summer before, when Mom approached me about having some tutoring, I was an emotional mess. I wanted to be okay, smart, and accomplished—without outside help. But, I was humbled, and after a summer of math classes, God had changed my heart about school. It was to be a joy—a time to learn and grow in knowledge, and be challenged. I set goals and worked through them, earnestly trying to redirect my eyes towards Jesus when the complaining spirit of my flesh erupted. I discovered that I was not really in the school of math, English, chemistry. Instead, I was in the school of joy, diligence, and trust.

However, the true secret to my junior year of highschool was the time I spent with Jesus. It was quality time, discovering truths in the Bible, finding how the stories of the Bible all fit together, and memorizing verses to cling to. Truly, "You will seek Me and find Me, when you search for Me with all your heart" (Jeremiah 29:13).

One thing that I remember God really doing during this time was drawing out my spiritual gifts. At the time, they just seemed like a natural overflow of my time with Him and my desire to share in His ways. It became my passion to listen to others, care about others deeply, mentor others, and use my words to bless others. I believe that my spiritual gifts are serving and mercy. Now, it is so special to look back and see, "God, that was you! Those emotions and actions and desires were naturally outpouring from time with you!"

I love to journal. During my high school years, I remember dreaming and journaling about starting a girls camp to encourage young girls in their walk with the Lord. One day, my mom and I were in the van, and I shared this dream with her. To my surprise and delight, she loved the idea deeply and encouraged me to pursue it. For a few days in late summer of that year, our back porch was transformed into a multi-purpose area for a girls camp. We invited all the girls from our church and, for three days, talked about Jesus, built stronger relationships, and started all types of traditions. Each summer since then, the girls camp has grown and changed. It has been humbling to see the power of prayer; the years that I spent more time in prayer beforehand have been so much more full of God's presence and peace.

Since my senior year and graduation, so much has changed. I have struggled deeply with all the change that finishing high school and getting older has brought into my life. However, more than I ever experienced in high school, I have seen how much people around me just long to be loved. People love to have a loving and listening friend. Even if they come from a very different culture and live a very different lifestyle than I. Every heart has deep hurts. As I share a coffee with friends, talk with them before class, or email them and build trust, the stories and heartbreak come pouring out. The marriages or boyfriend/girlfriend relationships are falling apart, the families are broken and full of anger, and the harsh words people have spoken to them have left scars in their souls. I struggle against myself; I want to stay home in comfort and be surrounded by my family and in control of my schedule. But, God. Oh, but,

God is challenging me to love others. The words of Ann Voskamp that I read on her blog in 2013 have stayed with me:

> *Never doubt that there's a love letter to bind up all the brokenhearted and it's signed with the scars of the Wounded God. Lay your weary head down on it, feed on it, break it, and share it with all the hurting world, everywhere you go. Love is always good news.* (www.aholyexperience.com)

People love to be loved. God is glorified when we love others — *No man hath seen God at any time. If we love one another, God dwelleth in us, and his love is perfected in us* (1 John 4:12). God is leading me to use my life, education, and everything in me to love, to cling to the love letter of God myself, to work through the struggles I have, to die to my flesh. And then, to lead the world around me to Him. It is hard, and I am in the thick of the fight against flesh. I still cry on my way to work sometimes because of the ache in my heart about leaving the wonderful, loving, beautiful family I have at home and going into the ugly, rude, dying world.

God has been so faithful to me and humbled me over and over. When I least expect it, I find myself in positions to share His love with others — when a coworker pulls me aside to tell me that she has a serious health problem and then to ask me to pray for her. When

I see a friend and just invite her to sit and talk with me, and, by the end of our conversation, she is saying, "This conversation is the reason God brought me here. I needed this." And I am sitting there thinking, "God is so loving!"

I have mulled over the question so many times, "What am I going to do with my future?" The answer I have received is so different than what I had thought. I am not focused on having a job as a nurse, a teacher, a photographer, or whatever it may be. That is not to be the purpose of my life, but, instead, an avenue. Life is about loving others out of the love God has poured into our hearts! Just as math, English, and chemistry were avenues for learning joy and diligence, so the path continues here! My profession, my job, the things I accomplish are simply avenues—opportunities to meet people, to love broken hearts, and to faithfully learn to share the Good News of the Love Letter of our Dear God!

Jessica Deagle

After I graduated from high school, I went through a period of searching and inquiring of the Lord. I enrolled in college as a nursing major, and the experience was challenging. I was away from home and felt alone. I loved music and longingly watched the music majors take off to their (what I imagined) wonderfully easy and lovely classes while I trudged off to the science building for a smelly lab class in chemistry. Yet I continued to press into the Lord.

During periods of loneliness and frustration, I have found that the answer is always—press into God. I began to spend even more time in His presence, reading my Bible, journaling prayers and answers to prayers. It was not the lighthearted college experience I had imagined. Although I had the occasional night of running out to the Waffle House at 2 am with friends, most of my days and nights were spent seeking direction for my life. I was still involved. I had friendships, I sang with a touring acapella group, and I participated in things, but my focus was on growing in God.

I desperately wanted to hear from the Lord. I wanted to know my next step. The Bible tells us that the steps of a righteous man are ORDERED of the Lord. More than anything, I had a desire for God to order my steps. My friendships were with those who would cause me to hunger more after the Lord. The books I read were those of others who had gone before me, seeking after the Father just as I was. I sat on my dorm-room bed and read Elisabeth Elliot's *Passion and Purity*. I read Amy Carmichael's biography, *A Chance to Die* in which a young girl's dreams of fame, singing, and theatre began to change into a woman's desire for love and a life consecrated completely to the Father God. I was growing. Ambition from the world's sense began to wane, and my hunger for the things of God began to grow. This was preparation time.

Of course I dreamed of love. He would be a man after God's own heart, alive with spiritual fervor . . . handsome, strong . . . perfect? Where was he?

After graduating from college and then nursing school, I learned of an opportunity through my church to go to Honduras. I was so excited! Yet part of me realized, here was a chance to die—a chance to die to the thought of finally dating, a chance to die to the idea of a cute apartment in the city while working at a nearby hospital, a chance to die to the comforts of life now with a college degree and some independence. Yet for me, it was truly a chance to live—I was ready for a challenge and bursting to be used. The idea of remaining single was daunting, but I sacrificed it on the altar of my desire to actually do something for God. My trunks were packed for Honduras . . . and more loneliness and searching.

But God is faithful! In Honduras, the Lord led me into more of Himself as I became acquainted with His Holy Spirit. I also met my husband there and was married shortly thereafter. I rejoice in the years of pressing into God, for I will need that experience in the years to come as a wife, mother, and home educator. Our years of preparation are never wasted, so, young women, draw near to God and watch Him eagerly draw near to you and set your life on a supernatural course (James 4:7)!

SUCH A TIME

Who knows but that you have come to your
royal position for such a time as this?
~Esther 4:14~

As we I begin the final chapter, I want to share with you the story of Esther. She was my favorite "princess" growing up. I even changed my middle name from "Eve" to "Esther" for a whole thirty-three days. She lived with passion, vision, and purpose, and it's from her story I coined the term *such a time*.

Esther was a young Jewess who was exiled with her people in Babylon when the king decided to select a new queen. All the beautiful and eligible women throughout the four corners of the known world were gathered to Susa. Of all the women, Esther found favor with everyone she met, including the king, who made her his queen.

Not long after her coronation, she received news from her uncle, who had raised her, that an irrevocable law had been issued that on the 13th day of the 12th month, the month of Adar — all the Jews would be killed.

Mordecai begged her to approach the king on behalf of her people. And Esther reminded her uncle that to approach the king unsummoned was certain death, unless the king extended his scepter. To this, Mordecai responded, "It may be that you have come to this position for such a time as this."

After fasting and praying for three days and three nights, Esther's maids prepared her to approach the king. Black coal outlined her eyes, making them sparkle like the stars in the sky. Draped in a brilliant turquoise material with delicate beadwork tracing the hem and the royal crown cradled in her silky black hair, her beauty was unrivaled, even by Vashti, whom she had replaced as queen.

Entering the throne room, she was met by an outstretched scepter. She continued to walk in the favor of God and the king. Several nights later, at a banquet she hosted for the king, she presented her request.

If I have found favor with you, Your Majesty, and if it pleases you, grant me my life — this is my petition. And spare my people — this is my request. For I and my people have been sold to be destroyed, killed and annihilated. If we had merely been sold as male and

> female slaves, I would have kept quiet, because no such distress would justify disturbing the king. (Esther 7:2-4)

I could be wrong, but I hardly think Esther was waiting all her life for this moment, that all her life, she dreamed of being imprisoned in the king's harem, to be selected as queen after twelve months, so that when she and her people were sentenced to death, she could save them. Instead, I would be willing to bet that it just happened, so she had to seize the moment and invest what had been placed in her lap to the best of her ability.

Esther lived *such a time* by taking what God had given her and walking with passion, vision, and purpose. That's also how you and I live for *such a time* as this — not waiting for tomorrow or to have all our "ducks in a row," But taking advantage of the moment and living today with passion, vision, and purpose no matter the day, no matter the circumstances, and no matter what others think.

Passion

Dictionary.com describes passion as "a powerful or compelling emotion; a strong or extravagant enthusiasm." In other words: an obsession; motivation to get out of bed in the morning; reason to exist; desire to thrive! I think Mr. Anonymous said it best, "Find something worth dying for, and then live for it." When we live for something, we're willing to die for—that's passion.

When passionate people come to my mind, I think of people like Mother Theresa, Jim Elliot, and Bethany Hamilton. They are all individuals who overcame great odds and accomplished astounding feats—people who changed the world. They were all driven by a passion: Mother Theresa was willing to die loving people; Jim Elliot was willing to die introducing secluded tribes to the gospel; and Bethany Hamilton was willing to die while becoming a great surfer. They had a clear passion and lived it—passion in motion.

Mother Theresa is one of my favorite examples of passion in motion. After serving as a nun for several years and being a teacher, the Lord burdened her heart for the destitute of Calcutta. Her heart's desire was to obey the Lord and serve Him. This desire led her to give up everything she had ever known and live among the poor in soul and possessions.

She said, "I am a little pencil in the hand of a writing God sending a love letter to His world." Her daily motivation to get out of bed was letting the Lord love people through her. It didn't matter to her if the price was humiliation or her personal health. Her passion to love not only changed the lives of forgotten individuals, but also represented what true love and real life are.

Vision

Know where you're going because lots of people are going nowhere fast, so . . . live for something worth dying for, but make sure you *know where you're going.* Passion is great, but if your passion is to go in circles, no one really cares and no one benefits; unless, of course, you benefit from getting dizzy . . .

Have a destination in mind. Envision the completed masterpiece. Visualize the goal.

I don't generally consider myself an artist. But hosting an event is a different story. I love mobilizing a team to transform a random space into a new world. My favorite experience of this is when I decorated for a "Dr. Suess" themed ball for youth from ages 12–21. Entering the gym of an old, run-down school-turned-church at 4 pm with ten willing workers, we knew we had our work cut out for us.

First we carried five boxes of decorations into the building, followed by twelve lampposts, paper, markers, scissors, twinkle lights, and stacks and stacks of Dr. Seuss books. Moving curtains, setting up tables, and arranging chairs consumed the next thirty minutes. Then, I decorated tables while my sisters created life-size posters of "Thing 1" and "Thing 2."

Buried in safety pins, posters, tablecloths, and Dr. Suess books, I didn't check the time again until my stomach rumbled. To my surprise, it was already 9:15 pm! No wonder it was dark outside, and I wanted to eat a family-size bag of potato chips all by myself. Looking up, I knew our mission had been accomplished. All we needed to do was tidy up and call it a day. Quickly, we wrapped up and headed home.

The next night, wearing tiaras and tuxes, we stepped into the world of Dr. Seuss. My vision of transforming a gym-turned-sanctuary into a Dr. Suess wonderland was a success. Creating a team and collecting decorations paid off, even if it did take us six hours. But none of it would have been possible if I hadn't picked a theme or thought ahead to gather things to make the theme come alive.

Can you imagine if I had shown up with no helpers, no decorations, no theme, and said, "Here I am. Now what?" The cold walls with chipped paint and mounted basketball hoops would have provided no direction and little inspiration. The world of "Dr. Seuss" would have been completely impossible without the vision. Even if I had all the willing workers, lampposts, and posters, they would have had little meaning unless I knew what I was trying to do: transform said space into the world of Dr. Seuss.

SUCH A TIME

It's the same in life. We can walk into it and say, "Here I am." Or we can walk into it and say, "There you are." Just as I knew what my facility consisted of before arriving at 4 pm, we know what we're dealing with in life: time, people, and circumstances.

Without a vision, we are asking time, people, or circumstances to tell us what to do. Occasionally, they will point in a random direction, so you'll wander around for a little bit, trying to decide if their idea is something you can be passionate about. Soon, you'll find that it's not exactly something you are willing to die for, so you find another clock, individual, or event to direct you. But, more often than not, they have no answer or direction. We're talking to a wall.

Stepping into life with vision puts us in charge. We walk up to a wall and announce, "There you are! I've been waiting to transform you, and I know just what you'll become." Just like an artist, you may not have all the details and exact pallet determined, but you know what you want the masterpiece to be. Before too long, the wall becomes a mural communicating your passion to everyone who walks by.

Instead of waiting for time, people, and circumstances to tell you what to do, which will lead you in circles, you decide. It doesn't mean that your ideas can't grow or even change, but at least having an idea puts you in a place to branch out. Like a tree, you can't have branches until you have a trunk.

When I started decorating for the "Dr. Seuss" ball, the furthest my vision had gone was: Dr. Suess books on the tables with tablecloths, lampposts around the room, and road signs taped to the lampposts. Hopefully, someone would bring a Dr. Seuss hat, but that didn't happen . . .

Before we left at 10 pm, we had a bike, the pants that walked by themselves, Thing 1 and Thing 2, twinkle lights throughout the room, and several of those extra fluffy, extra tall, extraordinary bird things hung up on the walls.

Passion in motion is useless if all it's doing is going in circles. Your vision determines the direction of your motion. Determine where you're going and go like you're going to die if you don't make it there.

Purpose

Passion puts us in motion and vision gives us direction, but what about when our passion runs out and we lose sight of the finish line? Then what? . . . Then, we need a *why* – a why that's bigger than our passion, bigger than our vision, and bigger than us. Because, let's face it, no matter how glorious our passion might be, there are going to be days when it just doesn't feel worth it or possible. That's when our *why* needs to focus our vision and give our passion a push.

As long as I can remember, I have wanted to run a women's ministry and mentor young women. Over the years, the vision and desire have changed a little, but the desire to minister and mentor remained.

Just a few months ago, as I was writing this book, I suddenly no longer wanted to host conferences and minister to women. Instead, I wanted to become a mobilization specialist (someone who specializes in team dynamics, building, and utilizing) and train corporate executives and military leaders how to lead successful teams. Wrestling with these polar-opposite thoughts, I remembered a question posed by Lara Casey in her book *Make It Happen*:

Who will be impacted by what you are doing?

That's when it dawned on me: my desire to minister and mentor wasn't my own. I had been impacted by the ministry of others and wanted to pour into others in a similar way out of the restoration and strength God had used others to give me. God had given me the passion. If God had given me a desire to encourage others through speaking and writing, it was because He had given me something to say that others need to hear.

If I didn't persevere and follow through with my dream, I would be robbing God, families, and myself: robbing God, of the glory He deserved; robbing families, of the message God created me to share with them; and robbing myself, from experiencing the fullness and faithfulness of God.

Writing this book really has nothing to do with me. And, thank goodness, because if it did, I would have stopped along time ago. My passion wasn't strong enough, and my vision wasn't clear enough. The stories I share in these chapters aren't to prove how perfect I am and how I have expertly navigated life.

If anything, hopefully you see the fingerprints of the Potter's hands as He makes my broken and warped self more like Him. Because that's the purpose of my living, the purpose of my writing, my *such a time* — to let others see through my brokenness to God's strength that holds me together.

"Such a Time" In Action

My passion is to minister and motivate. My vision is to have a ministry where I speak, write, host conferences, and mentor interns. My purpose is to inspire others to embrace their authentic identity and astounding potential in Jesus Christ; this clarifies my vision and motivates my passion. But I'm not waiting for *someday when.* I've started today. I'm not waiting until I have a website with my name and photo plastered on it or an inbox full of speaking requests.

I teach dance every week and remind my girls that the reason we dance is to glorify God by worshiping God, focusing on God, and helping others see God. I pray for my siblings and write them encouraging notes reminding them of who they are in Christ. I'm a contributor to *InsideOut*, an online Christian magazine. I work for my father as his office manager. I run a ballroom dance ministry for youth, equipping them with social ballroom and etiquette skills. And, I coordinate TeenPact Leadership Schools for the state of Virginia.

I love what Carolyn McCulley says in her book, *Did I Kiss Marriage Goodbye?*:

> "Am I called to singleness?" I've been asked that question several times, although no one asked until I reached my late thirties. I still don't know how to answer. Honestly, I don't know if one can apply that phrase to singleness. We're all *born* single; so don't we have to be called to something different? In my opinion, the question is not whether we're called to singleness but whether we're called to marriage.

Elisabeth Elliot put it this way in *Quest for Love*:

If you are single today, the portion assigned to you for today is singleness. It is God's gift. Singleness ought not to be viewed as a problem, nor marriage as a right. God in His wisdom and love grants either as a gift.

I wonder what life would look like, what women would look like, what our culture would look like, if we decided that we are called to today. Whatever that state may be—single or married, college student or office manager, sister or mom, dancer or athlete, drummer or harpist—let us live it for *such a time* as this.

The Dare

It's funny how much you learn when you write a book. I thought I understood this concept of *such a time* pretty well. I mean I hosted a conference about it, wrote about it here and there, even talked about it to an audience. But when it came to write about it, I realized how much more there was for me to learn on this topic of *such a time*. The biggest thing I have learned is that singleness is NOT about us.

As I have written and rewritten each chapter, I have been overwhelmed with my selfishness. Girls, singleness is not about us. Marriage is not about us. Not a single part of it. Having children has nothing to do with us.

SUCH A TIME

Single, married, or mother is all about God. It's all a talent we have been given to make His name known.

When we live for *someday when* like Rapunzel, with no passion, vision, or purpose, we are living for ourselves. Of this, I'm guilty. I am guilty of selfishly living for *someday when*, thinking that this life is all about me and making me happy, successful, and changing my last name. And, more than anything else, I want you to know that this selfish life of living for *someday when* has left me feeling empty and purposeless.

I cannot begin to describe to you the overwhelming discontentment, frustration, and rebellion that swirl in my heart when I live singleness for myself or for *someday when*.

But when I choose to live for *such a time*. When I take my eyes off of myself and live this life selflessly, as though I am investing it for my Creator, everything changes. I feel alive. I feel purposeful. I am able to love and serve and not care about when Prince Charming will come and change my last name or whose eyes my children will have. Instead, I feel like my life is important. I feel like Esther. I feel like I'm living for *such a time*.

Just like me, your *such a time* doesn't begin when you become a mommy or land that perfect dream job or even when you finally get a new last name—it's today. Your *such a time* is now. Joyce Meyer said, "God created you on purpose for a purpose." He gave you a vision to accomplish your purpose and passion to carry out that vision, which was inspired by the purpose God created you for.

Esther, Lindsey, Mother Theresa, Lydia, myself, and the countless other girls whose stories you've read throughout this book aren't super heroes. We're simply girls who accepted the dare. We're determined to look back on our lives with satisfaction. We don't want to miss the wedding feast like the seven maidens who didn't fill their oil lamps. And we don't want the Master to throw us out because we buried our talent instead of investing it.

We're passionate. We have a vision. And, we're living on purpose! Will you join us in living of life of *passion, vision,* and *purpose*?

SUCH A TIME
A DARE to live a life of memories instead of regrets,
An OPPORTUNITY to invest in others,
And a RESPONSIBILITY to glorify God.

REFLECT

Read the story of Esther: Esther 1–2:18, 3–5:8, 7–8:2, 8:15–17.

What is your passion? What are you most excited about or motivated by? What are you willing to die for?

What is your vision? How does living for what you're willing to die for look?

What is your purpose, your *why*, the reason that picks you back up when no one else cares?

What is your *SUCH A TIME*?

ABOUT THE AUTHOR

Samantha Roose is the founder of "Such A Time," a conference inspiring women to live with passion, vision, and purpose. She is also a life coach, dance instructor, personal trainer, triathlete, professional harpist, as well as the executive director and director of student leadership for The Great Dance, a ballroom dance ministry for youth. She has been mentoring those around her in life, fitness, healthy eating, music, dance, and relationships since 2010. Samantha Roose is a homeschool graduate, residing in Virginia with her family of 14, and shares 3 cars with 5 drivers. She is passionate about inspiring others to embrace their extraordinary identity and potential in Jesus Christ. If you want to find out more about Samantha's "Such A Time" conference (suchatimeconference.com) or let her know how her book has contributed to your life, you can contact her via email, samantharoosespeaks@gmail.com, or through Facebook, Pinterest, or Instagram.